Pocket Rough Guide

MADRID

written and researched by

SIMON BASKETT

Contents

INTRODUCTION TO

MADRID

The sunniest, highest and liveliest capital city in Europe, Madrid has a lot to take pride in. Indeed, its inhabitants, the Madrileños, are so proud of their city that they modestly declare "desde Madrid al Cielo": that after Madrid there is only one remaining destination – Heaven. While their claim may be open to dispute, this compact, frenetic and fascinating city certainly has bags of appeal and its range of attractions has made it a deservedly popular short-break destination.

PALACIO REAL

Best places for tapas

There is a vast array of bars in Madrid, serving up tasty tapas: take a stroll around Huertas, La Latina, Chueca and Malasaña and you will stumble on some of the best. A few of our favourites are: *La Chata* (p.36), *El Tempranillo* (p.37), *Los Caracoles* (p.50), *La Toscana* (p.63), *Casa del Abuelo* (p.62) and *El Bocaito* (p.88).

King Felipe II plucked Madrid from provincial oblivion when he made it capital of the Spanish empire in 1561. The former garrison town enjoyed an initial Golden Age when literature and the arts flourished, but centuries of decline and political turmoil followed. However, with the death of the dictator Franco in 1975 and the return to democracy the city had a second burst of creativity, *La Movida Madrileña*, an outpouring of hedonistic, highly innovative and creative forces embodied by film director Pedro Almodóvar. In recent years Madrid has undergone a major facelift, with the opening of state-of-the-art extensions to the leading museums, the redevelopment of the river area and the pedestrianization of some of the historic streets in the centre.

The vast majority of the millions of visitors make a beeline for the Prado, the Reina Sofía and the Thyssen-Bornemisza, three magnificent galleries that give the city a weighty claim to being the "European capital of art". Of equal appeal to football fans is the presence of one of the world's most glamorous and successful clubs, Real Madrid. Aside from these heavy hitters, there's also a host of smaller museums, palaces and parks, not to mention some of the best tapas, bars and nightlife in Spain.

FLAMENCO

When to visit

Traditionally, Madrid has a typical **continental climate**, cold and dry in winter, and hot and dry in summer. There are usually two rainy periods, in October/November and any time from late March to early May. With temperatures soaring to over 40ºC in July and August, the best times to visit are generally **spring** and **autumn**, when the city is pleasantly warm. The short, sharp winter takes many visitors by surprise, but crisp, sunny days with clear blue skies compensate for the drop in temperature.

Although Madrid is increasingly falling into line with other European capitals, many places still shut down in **August** as its inhabitants head for the coast or countryside. Luckily for visitors, and those Madrileños who choose to remain, sights and museums remain open and nightlife takes on a momentum of its own.

Madrid's short but eventful history has left behind a mosaic of traditions, cultures and cuisines, and you soon realize it's the inhabitants who play a big part in the city's appeal. Despite the morale-sapping economic crisis, Madrileños still retain an almost insatiable appetite for enjoying themselves, whether it be hanging out in the cafés or on the summer *terrazas*, packing the lanes of the Rastro flea market, filling the restaurants or playing hard and late in the bars and clubs.. The nightlife for which Madrid is renowned is merely an extension of the Madrileño character and the capital's inhabitants consider other European cities positively dull by comparison with their own. The city centre is a mix of bustling, labyrinthine streets and peaceful squares, punctuated by historic architectural reminders of the past. As with many of its international counterparts, an influx of fast-food and coffee chains has challenged the once dominant local bars and restaurants, but in making the transition from provincial backwater just thirty years ago to major European capital today, Madrid has managed to preserve many key elements of its own stylish and quirky identity.

RETIRO PARK

MADRID AT A GLANCE

>> EATING

Eating out in Madrid is one of the highlights of any visit to the city. There's plenty to suit every pocket, from budget backstreet bars to high-class designer restaurants, and a bewildering range of cuisines encompassing tapas, traditional Madrileño and Spanish regional dishes. Lunch is taken late, with few Madrileños starting before 2pm, while dinner begins after 9pm. Opening hours can be flexible, with many bars and restaurants closing on Sunday evenings or Monday and for all or part of August. You should spend at least one evening sampling the tapas bars around Santa Ana/Huertas and La Latina. Chueca and Malasaña have some superb traditional bars and bright new restaurants, serving some of the most creative food in the city. The smarter district of Salamanca contains few bars of note, but some extremely good (and expensive) restaurants.

>> DRINKING

Madrid is packed with a variety of bars, cafés and *terrazas*. In fact they are a central feature of Madrileño life and hanging out in bars is one of the best, and most pleasant, ways to get the feel of the city and its people. The areas bordering Puerta del Sol, in and around Cava Baja and Plaza Chueca are some of the liveliest, but you can stumble across a great bar in almost every street in the city centre.

>> NIGHTLIFE

As you'd expect with a city whose inhabitants are known as the "gatos" (the cats), there's a huge variety of nightlife on offer in the Spanish capital. The mainstays of the Madrid scene are the *discobares*, which get going around 11pm and stay open till 3am. The flashier *discotecas* are rarely worth investigating until around 1 or 2am, although queues often build up quickly after this time. Alonso Martínez, Argüelles and Moncloa are student hangouts, Salamanca is for the wealthy and chic, while head for Malasaña and Chueca if you want to be at the cutting edge of trendiness. You'll find a more eclectic mix on offer in the streets around Sol and Santa Ana.

>> SHOPPING

Head for Gran Vía and Calle Preciados if you're looking for department and chain stores and for the streets around Plaza Mayor if you're on the hunt for traditional establishments. For fashion and designer labels, the smartest addresses are in Salamanca, but more alternative designers are in Malasaña and Chueca. Fans of street fashion will like the shops on C/Fuencarral. Most areas of the city have their own *mercados* (indoor markets) devoted mainly to food, but for the classic Madrileño shopping experience make your way to the flea market in the Rastro on a Sunday.

OUR RECOMMENDATIONS FOR WHERE TO EAT, DRINK AND SHOP ARE LISTED AT THE END OF EACH CHAPTER.

Day One in Madrid

1 The Prado > p.66–67. The Prado contains a fabulous array of masterpieces by artistic greats such as Bosch, El Greco, Titian, Rubens Velázquez and Goya.

2 The Retiro > p.72. Ward off any museum fatigue by freshening up with a stroll around beautiful Retiro park.

Lunch > p.77. Housed in the state-of-the-art CaixaForum exhibition space on Paseo del Arte, *Arturo* offers a creative €12 *menu del día* in designer surroundings.

3 The Palacio Real > p.38–39. Marvel at the magnificent, over-the-top decor in this one-time royal residence now used only for ceremonial purposes.

Coffee > p.44. Looking out over the plaza towards the royal palace, the elegant *Café de Oriente* makes a great place for a relaxing drink.

4 Plaza Mayor > p.28. Built when the city became Spain's capital in the sixteenth century, Madrid's atmospheric main square retains an aura of traditional elegance.

5 Madrid de los Austrias > p.28. Take a step back in time and explore the twisting streets of ancient Madrid around La Latina.

Dinner > p.62–63. Hit the tapas trail around Huertas. Hop from bar to bar, sampling local specialities. *Casa Alberto, La Trucha* and *El Abuelo* are good places to make a start.

6 Flamenco > p.51. Finish the night off with some authentic flamenco at *Casa Patas*.

Day Two in Madrid

1 The Thyssen > p.72. An outstanding art collection assembled by the Thyssen-Bornemisza dynasty and providing an unprecedented excursion through Western art.

2 The Santiago Bernabéu > p.93. Home to the all-star Real Madrid, a tour of this awesome stadium is a must for any football fan. Better still, take in a game.

Lunch > p.88. Prepare yourself for a spot of shopping in Chueca and Malasaña by sampling a mouth-watering range of tapas at *El Bocaito*.

3 Shopping > p.85. Chueca and Malasaña are home to some of the city's hippest fashion outlets and most interesting independent stores.

4 Reina Sofía > p.70. An impressive home for Spain's collection of contemporary art, worth the visit if only to see Picasso's *Guernica*.

5 Gourmet Experience > p.88. Take in some of the best views in Madrid from the terrace bars on the ninth floor of El Corte Inglés in Callao.

Dinner > p.34. *El Botin* is reputedly the oldest *meson* in the city and serves up superb, traditional Castillian fare.

6 Club > p.45. Work off some calories with a dance at one of Madrid's clubs. *Joy Madrid* has an eclectic mix of music, a fun atmosphere and a fantastic setting for a late-night drink.

ITINERARIES

9

Budget Madrid

Many of Madrid's biggest sights are free at certain times of the week, while others charge no entry free at all. Here are some suggestions on how to spend a great day without spending a penny on anything, apart from food and drink.

1 Museo de los Orígenes > p.33. Housed in a sixteenth-century mansion that was supposedly once home to the city's patron saint, this museum traces the early history of the Spanish capital.

2 Iglesia de San Andrés > p.33. Next door to the Museo de Orígenes, this beautiful church and its adjoining chapels have been tastefully restored to their former glory.

Lunch > p.87 & p.60. With a great three-course set lunch menu for under €10, the *Gloria de Montera* and its sister restaurant *La Finca de Susana* are two of the best-value restaurants in the city.

4 Templo de Debod > p.102. Shipped stone by stone from the banks of the River Nile, this ancient Egyptian temple is an incongruous sight in the city. The little exhibition inside is free.

5 The Prado > p.66. Head here between 6 and 8pm on weekdays (Sun 5–7pm) and you'll see an unparalleled collection of art for nothing.

6 The Retiro > p.72. Take a stroll by the lake in the Retiro park to relax and unwind.

Dinner > p.106. The cheap and cheerful *Casa Mingo* serves some fantastic roast chicken and bottled cider.

3 Palacio Real > p.38. Visit the sumptuous palace on a Wednesday or Thursday afternoon and you'll get in for nothing – be prepared to queue.

7 Río Manzanares > Finish off the evening with a stroll by the redeveloped river area by the Puente de Segovia.

Off-the-beaten-track-Madrid

If you've got the time and have done the big sights, then why not take a break from the crowds and seek out some of Madrid's lesser-known, but highly rewarding attractions. Here are some of our suggestions.

1 Monasterio de las Descalzas Reales > p.42. Hidden behind an innocuous-looking door, this sixteenth-century convent is brimming full of artistic treasures.

2 San Francisco el Grande > p.33. Limited opening hours mean that this magnificent church and its frescoes are often overlooked.

3 Campo del Moro > p.41. Surprisingly under-visited, this English-style park below the Palacio Real provides a verdant retreat away from the bustle of the nearby streets.

4 Casa de Lope de Vega > p.53. Step back in time with a visit to this charming little museum in the house where the famous Golden Age dramatist once lived.

Lunch > p.78. Tucked away at the bottom of one of the little streets in Huertas, *La Vaca Verónica* serves an excellent *menú del día*.

5 Museo Nacional del Romanticismo > p.84. This delightful museum recreates bourgeois life in nineteenth-century Madrid.

6 Museo Sorolla > p.91. The artist's elegant former home provides the perfect setting for his luminescent paintings.

7 Lázaro Galdiano > p.93. Well off the tourist trail, this former private collection gets less than its fair share of attention and yet it houses an amazing cornucopia of art treasures.

Drink > p.99. Try out the little-known Plaza de Comendadoras and its *terrazas* for a pre-meal *aperitivo*.

Dinner > p.107. Just a handful of tables, but the tiny little *Toma* serves some tasty creative cuisine.

Big sights

1 Museo del Prado Quite simply one of the greatest art museums in the world. **>** **p.66**

2 Museo Thyssen-Bornemisza A superb collection of art put together by the Thyssen family and acting as a marvellous complement to the Prado. > **p.72**

4 Estadio Santiago Bernabéu
The Galácticos may have gone, but this magnificent stadium merits a visit even if you are unable to get to a game. > **p.93**

3 Palacio Real A sumptuous royal palace reflecting the past glories of the Spanish royal family. > **p.38**

5 Centro de Arte de Reina Sofía An essential stop on the art circuit, the Reina Sofía is home to Picasso's iconic masterpiece *Guernica*. > **p.70**

Eating out

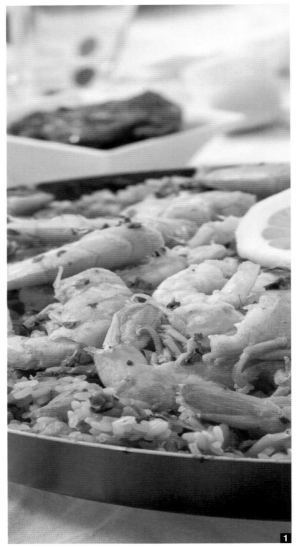

1 Regional dishes Madrid offers every regional style of Spanish cooking. Try *La Barraca* for an authentic Valencian paella. **> p.86**

2 Haute cuisine Ramón Freixa's flagship restaurant *Ramón Freixa Madrid* is one of Madrid's best new celebrity chef restaurants. ❯ **p.96**

3 Tapas For an authentic night out eating tapas, copy the locals and go bar-hopping in Huertas or La Latina. ❯ **p.50 & p.62**

4 Eating alfresco When you start to feel the heat, head outside to eat. The summer rooftop terrace at *Gaudeamus* has great views. ❯ **p.50**

5 Madrid specialities The meat and chickpea stew *cocido* is one of the city's traditional dishes – try it out at *Malacatín.* ❯ **p.50**

After dark

1 Bar culture Bars are a central feature of Madrileño life. The *Taberna Angel Sierra* on Plaza Chueca is a classic choice. **> p.89**

3 Cocktails Start or finish a Madrid night out with some cocktails. The stylish *Del Diego* serves up some of the best in town. > **p.88**

2 Flamenco Andalucía may be the home of flamenco, but Madrid has some top acts. *Casa Patas* is a favourite. > **p.51**

4 Clubbing Madrid has a massive range of clubs, from unpretentious *discobares* to serious cutting-edge dance venues. > **p.7**

5 Terrazas As temperatures soar, life moves outside and so do the bars – head for the *terrazas* in Plaza Santa Ana. > **p.64**

Museums and galleries

1 Real Fábrica de Tapices A fascinating museum and a thriving workshop, allowing visitors the chance to view works in progress. > **p.76**

3 Museo Sorolla The life and works of artist Joaquín Sorolla is housed in his lovely former residence. **> p.91**

2 Museo Arqueológico Nacional An impressive collection of Visigothic, Roman, Greek and Egyptian finds in a beautiful refurbished building next to Plaza Colón. **> p.91**

5 Museo Lázaro Galdiano A treasure-trove of paintings, furniture and *objets d'art* in this personal collection assembled by publisher and businessman José Lázaro Galdiano. **> p.93**

4 Real Academia de Bellas Artes It may not boast the heavyweight attractions of the big three, but this gallery contains some captivating work by Goya, El Greco, José de Ribera and Zurbarán. **> p.56**

Green spaces

1 **Casa de Campo** Once part of the royal hunting estate, Casa de Campo is the biggest and wildest of the city's parks. > **p.103**

2 The Retiro This city-centre park has become Madrileños' favourite playground, with a boating lake and a crystal palace hosting regular exhibitions. > **p.72**

3 Campo del Moro One of the city's most beautiful, and underused, parks with shady paths and ornamental pools. > **p.41**

5 Parque del Oeste The lovely Parque del Oeste contains assorted statues, a fragrant rose garden and even a genuine Egyptian temple. > **p.102**

4 Jardínes Botánicos Dating back to the eighteenth century, the botanical gardens form an amazingly tranquil oasis in the city. > **p.73**

23

Kids

1 Parque de Atracciones A popular theme park situated in Casa de Campo with a vast range of rides catering for all ages. **> p.104**

3 The Retiro The Retiro park has plenty of child-friendly attractions including play areas, puppet shows, duck ponds and a boating lake. > **p.72**

2 The Teleférico For a bird's-eye view of the city, take the cable car across the Manzanares river to Casa de Campo. > **p.103**

4 Madrid's Zoo Casa de Campo is home to an attractive zoo complete with lions, bears, koalas, sharks and many reptiles. > **p.104**

5 Museo de Ferrocarril With its model railways and array of full-size locomotives, this museum will be a hit with most children and many parents too. > **p.49**

PLACES

Madrid de los Austrias

Named after the royal family and their original homeland, the district known as Madrid de los Austrias, or Habsburg Madrid, is made up of some of the oldest and most atmospheric parts of the city. Centred around grandiose Plaza Mayor, the area is a twisting grid of streets, filled with Flemish-inspired architecture of red brick and grey stone. Most visitors only make it to the Plaza Mayor and its over-priced cafés and restaurants, but there are appealing sights scattered throughout the area, especially in the barrio (district) of La Latina, which stretches south of the square. This region is also home to some of the city's best restaurants, tapas bars and flamenco tablaos, especially around calles Almendro, Cava Baja and Cava Alta.

PLAZA MAYOR

Ⓜ **Sol.** MAP P.30–31, POCKET MAP C12

The splendidly theatrical Plaza Mayor was originally the brainchild of Felipe II who, in the late sixteenth century, wished to construct a more prestigious focus for his new capital. The Casa de la Panadería on the north side of the square is the oldest building, dating from 1590, but, like much of the plaza, it was rebuilt after fires in the seventeenth and eighteenth centuries. The gaudy frescoes that adorn the facade were only added in 1992. It now houses the municipal tourist office (daily 9.30am–8.30pm).

Capable of holding up to fifty thousand people, the square was used for state occasions, autos-de-fé (public trials of heretics followed, usually, by burning of the victims), plays and bullfights. The large bronze equestrian statue in the middle is of Felipe III and dates from 1616.

PLAZA MAYOR

Today, Plaza Mayor is primarily a tourist haunt, full of expensive outdoor cafés and restaurants. However, an air of grandeur clings to the plaza and it still hosts public functions, from outdoor theatre and music to Christmas fairs and a Sunday stamp and coin market.

CALLE MAYOR

Ⓜ Sol. MAP P.30–31, POCKET MAP A12–012

One of the oldest thoroughfares in the city, Calle Mayor was for centuries the route for religious processions from the Palacio Real to the Monastery of Los Jerónimos. The street is home to little shops and bars and is flanked by the facades of some of the most evocative buildings in the city. Set back from the road, near the entrance to the Plaza Mayor, is the splendid decorative ironwork of the **Mercado de San Miguel** (Sun–Wed 10am–midnight, Thurs–Sat 10am–2am; Ⓦ www .mercadodesanmiguel.es; see p.36). Built in 1916 it was formerly one of the old-style food markets scattered throughout the city, but it has now been refurbished and converted into a stylish tourist-oriented emporium complete with oyster and champagne bar.

SAN NICOLÁS DE LOS SERVITAS

Plaza de San Nicolás 1 Ⓜ Ópera. Tues–Sat 8.30–9.30am & 6.30–8.30pm. Sun & hols 10am–1.45pm & 6.30–8.45pm. MAP P.30–31, POCKET MAP A12

Largely rebuilt between the fifteenth and seventeenth centuries, Madrid's oldest church still includes a twelfth-century Mudéjar tower featuring traditional Arabic horseshoe arches. Juan de Herrera, architect of El Escorial (see p.116), is buried in the crypt.

STATUE OF ÁLVARO DE BAZÁN, PLAZA DE LA VILLA

PLAZA DE LA VILLA

Ⓜ Sol. MAP P.30–31, POCKET MAP A12

This charming plaza, just off Calle Mayor, showcases three centuries of Spanish architectural development. The oldest buildings are the simple but eye-catching fifteenth-century **Torre y Casa de Los Lujanes** where Francis I of France is said to have been imprisoned by Emperor Charles V after the Battle of Pavia in 1525. On the south side of the square is the **Casa de Cisneros**, constructed for the nephew of Cardinal Cisneros (early sixteenth-century Inquisitor-General and Regent of Spain) in the intricate Plateresque style.

The **Casa de la Villa** occupies the remaining side. An emblem of Habsburg Madrid, it was constructed in fits and starts from the mid-seventeenth century to house the offices and records of the council, who recently moved on to more grandiloquent headquarters in the Palacio de Cibeles. The initial design by Juan Gómez de Mora wasn't completed until 1693, 45 years after his death, and was mellowed by the addition of Baroque details in the eighteenth century.

RESTAURANTS

La Botillería de Maxi	16
El Botín	2
Casa Paco	4
ENE	9
El Estragón	7
La Musa Latina	11
Palacio de Anglona	5
Posada de la Villa	8

LIVE MUSIC

Las Carboneras	1
Corral de la Morería	2

TAPAS BARS

Almendro 13	13
Casa Revuelta	3
La Chata	12
Juana la Loca	20
Matritum	18
Mercado de San Miguel	1
Tapasentao	6
Txirimiri	21

BARS

Delic	15
María Pandora	14
El Tempranillo	17
El Ventorrillo	10
El Viajero	19

Madrid de los Austrias

ACCOMMODATION

Bed & Basic Abracadabra	7
Chic & Basic Mayerling	5
Hostal La Macarena	3
Hostal Tijcal	2
Hotel Plaza Mayor	4
Petit Palace Posada del Peine	1
Posada del León de Oro	6

SHOPPING

El Arco Artesania	4
Casa Yustas	1
Geppetto	2
La Librería	3
Lobo	5

PLAZA DE ISABEL II · ÓPERA

CALLE LAS HILERAS · CALLE ARENAL

San Ginés

PLAZA HERRADORES

CALLE MAYOR

PLAZA SAN MIGUEL

PLAZA MAYOR

PL. DEL CONDE DE MIRANDA

San Miguel

PLAZA PUERTA CERRADA

PLAZA SEGOVIA NUEVA

CALLE SEGOVIA

CALLE NUNCIO

ALMENDRO

CALLE CAVA BAJA

CALLE CAVA ALTA

CALLE TOLEDO

Iglesia Colegiata de San Isidro

CALLE COLEGIATA

Palacio de Santa Cruz

CALLE LA CONCEPCIÓN JERÓNIMA

TIRSO DE MOLINA

PLAZA DE TIRSO DE MOLINA

PL. DUQUE DE ALBA

CALLE DUQUE DE ALBA

Mercado del Rastro

CALLE JUANELO

CEBADA

Mercado de la Cebada

LA LATINA

PLAZA CASCORRO

C/ENCOMIENDA

C/RUDA

RIBERA DE CURTIDORES

Mercado del Rastro

SIERPE

CALLE SANTA ANA

PLAZA DEL GENERAL VARA DEL REY

N

0	metres	100
0	yards	100

31

PARQUE EMIR MOHAMED I

Ópera. MAP P.30–31, POCKET MAP B6

It is easy to miss this small, enclosed park opposite the crypt, but it is notable for the fragments of the city walls that date back to the ninth and twelfth centuries. The park lies on the Cuesta de la Vega, former site of one of the main entrances to Muslim Madrid, while nearby, the narrow, labyrinthine streets of the former Moorish quarter, La Morería, are still clearly laid out on medieval lines.

CONVENTO DE LAS CARBONERAS

Plaza Conde de Miranda 3 Sol. MAP P.30–31, POCKET MAP B13

Founded in the early seventeenth century, this convent belongs to the closed Hieronymite Order. It's famous for its home-made biscuits and cakes – a tradition in Spanish convents since the time of St Teresa de Ávila, who gave out sweetened egg yolks to the poor – which can be purchased every day (9.30am–1pm & 4–6.30pm). Ring the bell above the sign reading *venta de dulces* to be let in, then follow the signs to the *torno*; the business takes place by means of a revolving drum to preserve the closed nature of the order.

BASÍLICA DE SAN MIGUEL

C/San Justo 4 La Latina or Sol. July to mid-Sept Mon–Sat 10am–1.15pm & 6–9.15pm, Sun 9.45am–1.30pm & 6.30–9.15pm; mid-Sept to June Mon–Sat 9.45am–1.30pm & 5.30–9pm, Sun 9.45am–2.15pm & 6–9.15pm. MAP P.30–31, POCKET MAP B13

Standing among a host of other graceful buildings – most of which house local government offices – San Miguel stands out as one of the few examples of a full-blown Baroque church in Madrid. Designed at the end of the seventeenth century for Don Luis, the precocious 5-year-old Archbishop of Toledo and youngest son of Felipe V, its features include an unconventional convex facade with four recesses, each containing a statue, variously representing Charity, Strength, Faith and Hope.

SAN PEDRO EL VIEJO

Costanilla de San Pedro La Latina. Mon–Sat 9am–noon & 6–8pm, Sun 9am–1pm. MAP P.30–31, POCKET MAP B13

At the heart of busy La Latina is the Mudéjar tower of San Pedro El Viejo. The second-oldest church in Madrid, it's said to have been founded in the fourteenth century by Alfonso XI, and stands on the site of an old mosque, though most of the church was rebuilt in the seventeenth century.

PLAZA DE LA PAJA

La Latina. MAP P.30–31, POCKET MAP A14

One of the real gems of old Madrid, this ancient sloping plaza was the commercial and civic hub of the city before the construction of the Plaza Mayor, and was once surrounded by a series of mansions owned by local dignitaries. With the restored houses beaming down on the former market square, this is a rare peaceful and traffic-free spot in the city. At the

PLAZA DE LA PAJA

bottom is the pretty little Jardín del Príncipe de Anglona (daily: winter 10am–6.30pm; summer 10am–10pm), a survivor of the gardens that used to be attached to the nearby mansions.

IGLESIA DE SAN ANDRÉS, CAPILLA DEL OBISPO AND CAPILLA DE SAN ISIDRO

Plaza de San Andrés ⓂLa Latina. Mon–Thurs & Sat 8am–1pm & 6–8pm, Fri 6–8pm, Sun 9am–2pm. MAP P.30–31, POCKET MAP A14

The Iglesia de San Andrés was badly damaged by an anarchist attack in 1936, and the adjoining Gothic Capilla del Obispo (guided tours Tues 10am–12.30pm & Thurs 4–5.30pm; reservation only on ☎915 592 874; €2), with its polychromed altarpiece and alabaster tombs, was only recently reopened following a forty-year restoration. The main church and the Baroque Capilla de San Isidro are reached by walking round the building into Plaza de San Andrés. The chapel was built in the mid-seventeenth century to hold the remains of Madrid's patron saint, San Isidro (since moved to the Iglesia de San Isidro), and the interior features a beautifully sculpted dome.

MUSEO DE LOS ORÍGENES

Plaza de San Andrés 2 ⓂLa Latina. Tues–Sun 9.30am–8pm. Free. MAP P.30–31, POCKET MAP A14

Housed in a reconstructed sixteenth-century mansion – supposedly home to San Isidro – this museum includes an exhibition on the history of Madrid. The city's archeological collection is in the basement, while the rest of the building is given over to the saint himself, with displays relating to his life and miraculous activities. The house also contains a well, site of one of Isidro's most famous exploits: he rescued his young

IGLESIA DE SAN ANDRÉS

son from the murky depths, by praying until the waters rose to the surface. The seventeenth-century chapel contained within the museum is built on the spot where the saint was said to have died in 1172.

SAN FRANCISCO EL GRANDE

Plaza de San Francisco 11 ⓂLa Latina. Tues–Sat 10.30am–1pm & 4–6.30pm (ticket office closes 6pm). €3 with guided tour. MAP P.30–31, POCKET MAP B7

Following a twenty-year restoration programme, you can appreciate this magnificent eighteenth-century domed church in something close to its original glory. Inside, each of the six chapels is designed in a distinct style ranging from Mozarab and Renaissance to Baroque and Neoclassical. Look out for the early Goya, *The Sermon of San Bernadino of Siena*, in the chapel on your immediate left as you enter, which contains a self-portrait of the 37-year-old artist (in the yellow suit on the right).

Even if your Spanish is not that good, follow the guided tour to get a glimpse of the church's other art treasures, including paintings by José de Ribera and Zurbarán.

Shops

EL ARCO ARTESANIA

Plaza Mayor 9 ⓂSol. Mon–Sat 11am–8pm, Sun 11am–2.30pm. MAP P.30–31, POCKET MAP B13

Though at the heart of tourist Madrid, the goods for sale here are a far cry from the swords, lace and castanets that fill most shops in the area. Crafts include ceramics, leather, wood, jewellery and textiles.

CASA YUSTAS

Plaza Mayor 30 ⓂSol. Mon–Sat 9.30am–9.30pm, Sun 11am–9.30pm. MAP P.30–31, POCKET MAP C12

Established in 1894, Madrid's oldest hat shop sells every conceivable model from pith helmets and commando berets to panamas and bowlers. There's also a large range of souvenir-style goods, including Lladró porcelain figurines.

GEPPETTO

C/Mayor 78 ⓂSol. Mon–Sat 10am–8.30pm. MAP P.30–31, POCKET MAP A12

Surrounded by a host of garish souvenir shops, this little place offers something quite different: handmade wooden toys and trinkets from Italy. Perfect if you're buying for a small child.

LA LIBRERÍA

C/Mayor 80 ⓂSol. Mon–Fri 10am–2pm & 4.30–7.30pm, Sat 11am–2pm. MAP P.30–31, POCKET MAP A12

Tiny place full of books just about Madrid. Most are in Spanish, but many would serve as coffee-table souvenirs. Also good for old prints of the city.

LOBO

C/Toledo 30 ⓂLa Latina. Mon–Fri 9.45am–1.45pm & 4.30–8pm, Sat 9.45am–1.45pm. MAP P.30–31, POCKET MAP C13

Great old-fashioned shoe shop, with anything from espadrilles to Menorcan sandals (€25) in every conceivable colour. Excellent for kids' shoes.

Restaurants

LA BOTILLERÍA DE MAXI

C/Cava Alta 4 ⓂLa Latina ☎ 913 651 249. Tues–Sat 12.30–4pm & 8.30pm–12.30am, Sun 12.30–6pm. Closed two weeks in Aug. MAP P.30–31, POCKET MAP B14

A mix of fine traditional staples and interesting new dishes. Specialities include the Madrid classic *callos* (tripe in tomato sauce) and *rabo de toro* (oxtail), but they also have international dishes such as Greek salad and Moroccan kebabs. A €10 lunch-time menu is available.

EL BOTÍN

C/Cuchilleros 17 ⓂSol ☎ 913 664 217. Daily 1–4pm & 8pm–midnight. MAP P.30–31, POCKET MAP C13

Established in 1725, the atmospheric *El Botín* is cited in the *Guinness Book of Records* as Europe's oldest restaurant. Favoured by Hemingway, it's inevitably a tourist haunt, but not such a bad one. Highlights are the Castilian roasts – especially *cochinillo* (suckling pig) and *cordero lechal* (lamb).

CASA YUSTAS

CASA PACO

Plaza Puerta Cerrada 11 🚇 La Latina
☎ 913 663 166. Mon–Sat 1.30–4pm &
8pm–midnight. Closed Aug. MAP P.30–31, POCKET
MAP B13

This classic, traditional
comedor, with no-nonsense
service, dishes out some of
the best meat dishes in town.
Specializes in sirloin steak
(*solomillo*), and another
delicious cut known as *cebón
de buey*. About €35 a head.

ENE

C/Nuncio 19 🚇 La Latina ☎ 913 662 591.
Mon–Wed 11am–11.30pm, Thurs open till
2am, Fri & Sat till 3am, Sun till midnight.
MAP P.30–31, POCKET MAP A14

Fashionable bar/restaurant just
below Plaza de la Paja serving
a fusion-style €11 *menú del día*
and a tasty but overpriced €22
brunch at weekends. Cocktails
and DJs Thurs–Sun.

EL ESTRAGÓN

Plaza de La Paja 10 🚇 La Latina
☎ 913 658 982. Daily 1–4pm &
8pm–midnight. MAP P.30–31, POCKET MAP A14

With a fine setting on this
ancient plaza, this cosy
vegetarian restaurant serves
hearty food; think stuffed
peppers, lasagne and paella. It
does a varied *menú del día* for
€8 (dinner *menú* €19), while
eating à la carte is pricier.

LA MUSA LATINA

Costanilla San Andrés 12 🚇 La Latina.
Mon & Tues 12.30pm–midnight, Thurs
12.30pm–12.30am, Fri 9am–2am, Sat
12.30pm–1am, Sun 1pm–midnight. MAP P.30–31,
POCKET MAP A14

Stylish place serving a great-
value €11 *menú del día*, and a
small selection of modern tapas
such as vegetable tempura,
fried green tomatoes and wok
dishes. It has a cool brick-
walled bar downstairs with DJ
sessions.

POSADA DE LA VILLA

PALACIO DE ANGLONA

C/Segovia 13 🚇 La Latina ☎ 913 653 153.
Tues–Thurs & Sun 9pm–1am, Fri & Sat till
2am. MAP P.30–31, POCKET MAP A13

Housed in the cellars of an
old mansion, this good-value
restaurant has imaginative
dishes (around €8–9 for mains)
such as oxtail hamburgers and
gazpacho with basil ice cream.
Good cocktails in the bar too.

POSADA DE LA VILLA

C/Cava Baja 9 🚇 La Latina ☎ 913 661 860.
Mon–Sat 1–4pm & 8pm–midnight,
Sun 1–4pm. Closed Aug. MAP P.30–31, POCKET
MAP B14

La Latina's most attractive
restaurant, spread over three
floors of a seventeenth-century
inn. Cooking is Madrileño,
including superb roast lamb.
Reckon on €45–50 per person.

Tapas bars

ALMENDRO 13

C/Almendro 13 🚇 La Latina. Mon–Fri 1–4pm
& 7.30pm–midnight, Sat, Sun & hols 1–5pm &
8pm–midnight. MAP P.30–31, POCKET MAP B14

Packed at weekends, this
fashionable wood-panelled bar
serves great *fino* sherry and
house specials of *huevos rotos*
(fried eggs on a bed of crisps)
and *roscas rellenas* (bread rings
stuffed with various meats).

LA CHATA

CASA REVUELTA

C/Latoneras 3 Ⓜ Sol or La Latina. Tues-Sat 1-4pm & 8pm-midnight, Sun 1-4pm. Closed Aug. MAP P.30-31, POCKET MAP C13

A timeless, down-to-earth little bar located in an alleyway just south of Plaza Mayor. It serves a melt-in-the-mouth tapa of *bacalao frito* (battered cod).

LA CHATA

C/Cava Baja 24 Ⓜ La Latina. Daily 2-4.30pm & 8.30pm-12.30am. Closed Tues & Wed lunchtime & Sun eve. MAP P.30-31, POCKET MAP B14

One of the city's most traditional and popular tiled tapas bars, with hams hanging from the ceiling and taurine memorabilia on the walls. Serves a good range of dishes, including excellent *rabo de toro* (oxtail) and *pimientos del piquillo rellenos* (stuffed onions and peppers).

JUANA LA LOCA

Plaza Puerta de Moros 4 Ⓜ La Latina. Tues-Sat noon-4.30pm & 8.30pm-1am, Sun noon-4.30pm. Closed Aug. MAP P.30-31, POCKET MAP C7

Fashionable hangout serving inventive tapas – tortilla with caramelized onion, tuna carpaccio, ostrich steaks – and a great selection of very tasty, but fairly pricey, canapés.

MATRITUM

C/Cava Alta 17 Ⓜ La Latina. Tues 8.30pm-midnight, Wed-Sun 1-4.30pm & 8.30pm-midnight. Closed Aug. MAP P.30-31, POCKET MAP B14

Delicious designer-style tapas, from scallops in a bacon and parmesan sauce to artichoke salad in mustard vinaigrette. There's a collection of carefully selected wines too.

MERCADO DE SAN MIGUEL

Plaza de San Miguel Ⓜ Sol. Sun-Wed 10am-midnight, Thurs-Sat 10am-2am. MAP P.30-31, POCKET MAP B12

Transformed from a neighbourhood market into a hip location for an *aperitivo*, this beautiful wrought-iron *mercado* is worth exploring at almost any time of day. There's something for everyone, from vermouth and champagne to salt cod, oysters and sushi.

TAPASENTAO

C/Príncipe Anglona Ⓜ La Latina. Mon-Fri noon-4pm & 8pm-midnight, Sat & Sun noon-1am. MAP P.30-31, POCKET MAP A14

Just opposite the church of San Pedro el Viejo, this popular bar serves up a wide range of interesting and original tapas, many of which are suitable for vegetarians. Favourites include crunchy, fried aubergines, vegetable tempura and battered mushrooms.

TXIRIMIRI

C/Humilladero 6 Ⓜ La Latina. Daily 12.30-4.30pm, 8.30pm-midnight. MAP P.30-31, POCKET MAP C7

Fantastic range of tapas and *pintxos* in this ever-popular bar beside the Mercado de la Cebada. Mouth-watering combinations include langoustine *croquetas*, mushroom risotto and their speciality, Unai hamburger.

Bars

DELIC

Costanilla San Andrés 14 ⓜ La Latina.
Mon 7pm–2am, Tues–Thurs & Sun
11am–2am, Fri & Sat 11am–2.30am. Closed
first half of Aug.
MAP P.30–31, POCKET MAP A14

Serving home-made cakes,
fruit juices and coffee, this
is a pleasant café by day,
transforming into a crowded but
friendly cocktail bar by night.

MARÍA PANDORA

Plaza Gabriel Miró 1 ⓜ La Latina.
Mon–Sat 7pm–2am, Sun 4pm–2am. Closed
second half of Aug. MAP P.30–31, POCKET MAP B7

An incongruous mix of
champagnería (champagne bar)
and library, where quality *cava*
can be enjoyed with the perfect
accompaniment of chocolates
and mellow jazz.

EL TEMPRANILLO

C/Cava Baja 38 ⓜ La Latina. Daily 1–4pm
& 9pm–2am. Closed two weeks in Aug.
MAP P.30–31, POCKET MAP B14

Popular little wine bar serving
a vast range of domestic
wines by the glass. A great
place to discover your favourite
Spanish *vino* – and the tapas
are excellent too.

EL VENTORRILLO

C/Bailén 14 ⓜ La Latina or Ópera.
Daily 11am–1am, Fri & Sat till 2am.
MAP P.30–31, POCKET MAP C7

This popular *terraza* is great for
a relaxing drink while enjoying
the *vistillas* (little views) over
the cathedral and mountains,
but avoid the over-priced tapas.

EL VIAJERO

Plaza de la Cebada 11 ⓜ La Latina. Tues–
Thurs 2pm–12.30am, Fri & Sat 2pm–1am, Sun
2–7pm. Closed first half Jan, second half Aug.
MAP P.30–31, POCKET MAP B14

Bar, club, restaurant and
summer *terraza* all in one,
spread over different floors
of this fashionable La Latina
nightspot. The food (meat,
pizza and pasta) is good too,
but pricey.

Live music

LAS CARBONERAS

Plaza Conde de Miranda ⓜ Sol
☎ 915 428 677, ⓦ www.tablaolascarboneras
.com. Mon–Sat: shows 8.30pm & 10.30pm (Fri
& Sat 11pm). MAP P.30–31, POCKET MAP B13

Geared up for the tourist
market, this *tablao* is gaining
a growing reputation on the
flamenco scene with a good
range of guest artists. At
around €70 with dinner it
remains slightly cheaper than
its rivals.

CORRAL DE LA MORERÍA

C/Morería 17 ⓜ La Latina or Ópera
☎ 913 658 446, ⓦ www.corraldelamoreria
.com. Daily 8pm–2am: shows at 9pm &
10.55pm. MAP P.30–31, POCKET MAP C7

An atmospheric, if expensive,
venue for serious flamenco
acts. Around €40 to see the
show and over double that
if you want to dine in the
restaurant as well.

CORRAL DE LA MORERÍA

Palacio Real and Ópera

Although the barrio only became fashionable in the mid-nineteenth century, the attractions found in the compact area around Ópera metro station date back as far as the 1500s. The imposing and suitably lavish Palacio Real (Royal Palace) dominates this part of the city, bordered by the somewhat disappointing Catedral de la Almudena and the tranquil gardens of the Campo del Moro. The restored Teatro Real and Plaza de Oriente bring some nineteenth-century sophistication to the area, while the two monastery complexes of la Encarnación and las Descalzas Reales conceal an astounding selection of artistic delights. For after-dark attractions, the area is home to one of the city's leading clubs as well as a handful of pleasant cafés and restaurants.

PALACIO REAL

C/Bailén ⓂÓpera or Sol Ⓦwww.patrimonio nacional.es. Daily: April–Sept 10am–8pm; Oct–March 10am–6pm; closed for state occasions and on Jan 1 & 6, May 1 & 15, Oct 12, Nov 9, Dec 24, 25 & 31. €10; free for EU citizens Mon–Thurs: Oct–March 4–6pm; April–Sept 6–8pm. MAP P.40, POCKET MAP C5

The present Palacio Real (Royal Palace) was built by Felipe V after the ninth-century Arab-built Alcázar was destroyed by fire in 1734. The Bourbon monarch, who had been brought up in the more luxurious surroundings of Versailles, took the opportunity to replace it with an altogether grander affair. He did not, however, live to see its completion and the palace only became habitable in 1764 during the reign of Carlos III. Nowadays it's used only for ceremonial purposes, with the present royal family preferring the more modest Zarzuela Palace, 15km northwest of the city.

The ostentation lacking in the palace's exterior is more than compensated for inside, with swirling marble floors, celestial frescoes and gold furnishings. It's a flamboyant display of wealth and power that was firmly at odds with Spain's declining status at the time. Look out for the grandiose **Salón del Trono**

THE PALACIO REAL

(Throne Room), the incredible oriental-style **Salón de Gasparini** (the Gasparini Room) and the marvellous **Sala de Porcelana** (Porcelain Room), decorated with one thousand gold, green and white interlocking pieces.

The palace outbuildings and annexes include the recently refurbished **Armería Real** (Royal Armoury), containing a fascinating collection of guns, swords and armour. There's also an eighteenth-century **farmacia** (pharmacy) and a **Galería de Pinturas** which displays works by Caravaggio, Velázquez and Goya and also hosts temporary exhibitions.

JARDINES DE SABATINI

Ⓜ Ópera. Daily: April–Sept 9am–10pm; Oct–March 9am–9pm. MAP P.40, POCKET MAP B4–C4

The Jardines de Sabatini (Sabatini Gardens) make an ideal place from which to view the northern facade of the palace or to watch the sun go down. They contain a small ornamental lake, some fragrant magnolia trees and manicured hedges, while, in summer, they're often used as a concert venue.

CATEDRAL DE LA ALMUDENA

Ⓜ Ópera. Daily: 9am–8.30pm, July & Aug 10am–9pm. Not open for visits during Mass: Mon–Sat noon, 6pm & 7pm, Sun & hols 10.30am, noon, 1.30pm, 6pm & 7pm. MAP P.40, POCKET MAP B6

Planned centuries ago, Madrid's cathedral, Nuestra Señora de la Almudena, was plagued by lack of funds, bombed in the Civil War and finally opened in 1993. More recently it was the venue for the wedding of the heir to the throne, Prince Felipe, and his former newsreader bride, Letizia Ortiz.

The cathedral's cold Gothic interior housed within its stark Neoclassical shell is not particularly inspiring, though the garish ceiling designs and the sixteenth-century altarpiece in the Almudena chapel are exceptions. To one side of the main facade is a small **museum** (Mon–Sat 10am–2.30pm; €6, €4 for Madrid residents and students) containing some of the cathedral's treasures, though the main reason to visit is to gain access to the dome from where you can enjoy some fantastic views over the city. The entrance to the **crypt** (daily 10am–2pm & 5–8pm) with its forest of columns and dimly lit chapels is on C/Mayor.

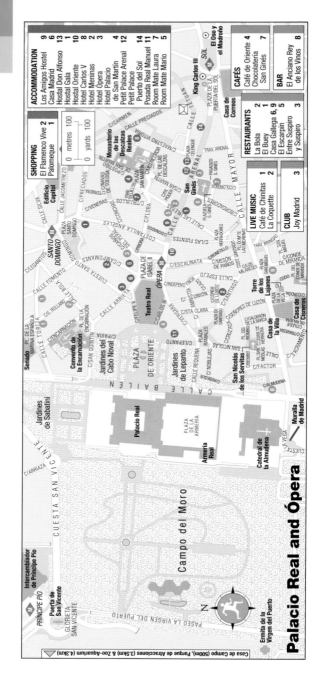

ACCOMMODATION

Los Amigos Hostel	9
Casa Madrid	6
Hostal Don Alfonso	13
Hostal Gala	1
Hostal Oriente	10
Hotel Carlos V	8
Hotel Meninas	2
Hotel Ópera	3
Hotel Palacio de San Martín	4
Petit Palace Arenal	12
Petit Palace	
Puerta del Sol	14
Posada Real Manuel	11
Room Mate Laura	7
Room Mate Mario	5

SHOPPING

El Flamenco Vive	2
Palomeque	1

CAFÉS

Café de Oriente	4
Chocolatería San Ginés	7

BAR

El Anciano Rey de los Vinos	8

RESTAURANTS

La Bola	2
El Buey	1
Casa Gallega	6, 9
El Escarpin	5
Entre Suspiro y Suspiro	3

LIVE MUSIC

Café de Chinitas	1
La Coqueta	2

CLUB

Joy Madrid	3

Palacio Real and Ópera

Casa de Campo (500m), Parque de Atracciones (3.5km) & Zoo-Aquarium (4.3km)

CAMPO DEL MORO

Entrance on Paseo de la Virgen del Puerto
Ⓜ Príncipe Pío. Daily: April–Sept 10am–8pm;
Oct–March 10am–6pm; closed occasionally
for state occasions. MAP P.40, POCKET MAP B5

One of the most underused
– largely because of its
inconvenient entrance down
by the river – and beautiful
of Madrid's parks, the Campo
del Moro gets its name from
being the site of the Moors'
encampment, from where,
in 1109, they mounted their
unsuccessful attempt to
reconquer Madrid. It later
became a venue for medieval
tournaments and celebrations.
After the building of the
Palacio Real several schemes
to landscape the area were put
forward, but it wasn't until
1842 that things got under way.
Based around two monumental
fountains, *Las Conchas* and
Los Tritones, the grassy gardens
are very English in style,
featuring shady paths and
ornamental pools, and provide
an excellent refuge from the
summer heat, as well as a
splendid view of the palace.

PLAZA DE ORIENTE

Ⓜ Ópera. MAP P.40, POCKET MAP A11

The aristocratic, pedestrianized
Plaza de Oriente is one of the
most attractive open spaces in
Madrid. The days when Franco
used to address crowds here
from the balcony of the royal
palace now seem a distant
memory, although a small
number of neo-Fascists still
gather here on the anniversary
of his death, November 21.

The fountain in the centre
was designed by Narciso
Pascual y Colomer, who also
transferred the bronze equestrian statue of Felipe IV here
from the garden of the Buen
Retiro Palace, near the Prado.
Dating from 1640, this statue is
reputedly the first-ever bronze
featuring a rearing horse –
Galileo is said to have helped
with the calculations to make
it balance. Other statues depict
Spanish kings and queens, and
were originally designed to
adorn the palace facade, but
were too heavy or, according
to one version, too ugly, and
were removed on the orders of
Queen Isabel Farnese.

There's a very French feel to
the buildings overlooking the
square, with their glass-fronted
balconies, underlined by the
elegant neo-Baroque *Café de
Oriente*, a favourite with the
opera crowd.

PLAZA DE ORIENTE

TEATRO REAL

Plaza de Isabel II Ⓜ Ópera ☎ 915 160 660, ticket line ☎ 902 244 848, Ⓦ www .teatro-real.com. Open for visits daily 10.30am–1pm; closed mid-July to mid-Sept; reservations ☎ 915 160 696. €8; tickets on sale 9.15am–1pm at the box office. MAP P.40, POCKET MAP A11–B11

When it opened in 1850, the hulking grey hexagonal opera house became the hub of fashionable Madrid and staged highly successful works by Verdi and Wagner. It fell into decay in the late twentieth century and after a ten-year refurbishment – that should have lasted four – and a staggering US$150 million in costs, it finally reopened in October 1997. With its lavish red and gold decor, crystal chandeliers, state-of-the-art lighting and superb acoustics it makes a truly magnificent setting for opera, ballet and classical concerts. Tickets range from €9 to €300, but you'll need to book well in advance for the best seats.

CONVENTO DE LA ENCARNACIÓN

Plaza de la Encarnación 1 Ⓜ Ópera Ⓦ www .patrimonionacional.es. Tours only (some in English) Tues–Sat 10am–2pm & 4–6.30pm, Sun & hols 10am–3pm. €7; joint ticket with Monasterio de las Descalzas Reales €10, valid for 48 hours; Wed free for EU citizens. MAP P.40, POCKET MAP A10

Founded in 1611 by Felipe III and his wife Margarita de Austria, this convent was intended as a retreat for titled women and merits a visit for its reliquary alone – one of the most important in the Catholic world. The solemn granite facade is the hallmark of architect Juan Gómez de Mora, also responsible for the Plaza Mayor. Much of the painting contained within is uninspiring, but there are some interesting items, including an extensive collection of royal portraits and a highly prized collection of sculptures of Christ. The library-like **reliquary** contains more than 1500 saintly relics from around the world: skulls, arms encased in beautifully ornate hand-shaped containers and bones from every conceivable part of the body. The most famous of the lot is a small glass bulb said to contain the blood of St Pantaleón – a fourth-century doctor martyr – which supposedly liquefies at midnight every July 26 (the eve of his feast day). Great tragedies are supposed to occur if the blood fails to liquefy. The tour ends with a visit to the Baroque-style church which features a beautifully frescoed ceiling and a marble-columned altarpiece.

MONASTERIO DE LAS DESCALZAS REALES

Plaza de las Descalzas 3 Ⓜ Callao, Sol or Ópera Ⓦ www.patrimonionacional.es. Tours only (some in English) Tues–Sat 10am–2pm & 4–6.30pm, Sun & hols 10am–3pm. €7; joint ticket with Convento de la Encarnación €10, valid for 48 hours; Wed free for EU citizens. MAP P.40, POCKET MAP C10–C11

One of the less well-known treasures of Madrid, the "Monastery of the Barefoot Royal Ladies" was originally the site of a medieval palace. The building was transformed by Juana de Austria into a convent in 1564, and the architect of El Escorial, Juan Bautista de Toledo, was entrusted with its design. Juana was the youngest daughter of the Emperor Charles V and, at the age of 19, already the widow of Prince Don Juan of Portugal. Royal approval meant that it soon became home to a succession of titled ladies who brought with them an array of artistic treasures, helping the convent accumulate a fabulous collection of paint-

MONASTERIO DE LAS DESCALZAS REALES

ings, sculptures and tapestries. The place is still unbelievably opulent and remains in use as a religious institution, housing 23 shoeless nuns of the Franciscan order.

The magnificent main staircase connects a two-levelled cloister, lined with small but richly embellished chapels, while the Tapestry Room contains an outstanding collection of early seventeenth-century Flemish tapestries based on designs by Rubens. The other highlight of the tour is the Joyería (Treasury), piled high with jewels and relics of uncertain provenance. Royal portraits and beautiful, wooden sculptures, most of unknown origin, decorate other rooms.

SAN GINÉS

C/Arenal 13 ⓂÓpera/Sol. Daily 8.15am–1pm & 6–9pm. Free. MAP P.40, POCKET MAP C11

Of Mozarabic origin (built by Christians under Moorish rule), this ancient church was completely reconstructed in the seventeenth century. There is an El Greco canvas of the moneychangers being chased from the temple in the Capilla del Cristo (on show Mon 12.30pm).

Shops

EL FLAMENCO VIVE

C/Conde de Lemos 7Ⓜ Ópera or Sol. Mon–Sat 10.30am–2pm & 5–9pm. MAP P.40, POCKET MAP B12

A fascinating little slice of Andalucía in Madrid, specializing in all things flamenco, from guitars and CDs to dresses and books.

PALOMEQUE

C/Arenal 17 Ⓜ Ópera or Sol. Mon–Sat 9.30am–1.30pm & 4.30–8pm, Sun 11am–8pm. MAP P.40, POCKET MAP C11

Founded back in 1873, this somewhat incongrous religious superstore has kept its place amongst the fashion outlets, hotels and restaurants that line this busy shopping street. Inside you'll find all manner of spiritual paraphernalia from elaborate alabaster altarpieces and sculptures of angels to rosary beads and postcard collections of Spanish saints and virgins.

Cafés

CAFÉ DE ORIENTE

Plaza de Oriente 2 Ⓜ Ópera. Mon–Thurs &
Sun 8.30am–1.30am, Fri & Sat till 2.30am.
MAP P.40, POCKET MAP A11

Elegant, Parisian-style café
with a popular *terraza* looking
across the plaza to the palace.
The café was opened in the
1980s by a priest, Padre
Lezama, who ploughs his
profits into various charitable
schemes. There's an equally
smart bar, *La Botilleria* (open
noon–1am, an hour later on Fri
& Sat), next door.

CHOCOLATERÍA SAN GINÉS

Pasadizo de San Ginés 11 Ⓜ Sol or Ópera.
Daily 9.30am–7am. MAP P.40, POCKET MAP C12

A Madrid institution, this café,
established in 1894, serves
chocolate con churros (thick
hot chocolate with deep-fried
hoops of batter) to perfection
– just the thing to finish off a
night of excess. It's an almost
compulsory Madrileño custom
to end up here after the clubs
close, before heading home for
a shower and then off to work.

Restaurants

LA BOLA

C/Bola 5 Ⓜ Santo Domingo or Ópera
☏ 915 476 930. Mon–Sat 1–4pm &
8.30–11pm, Sun 1–4pm. MAP P.40, POCKET
MAP A10

Opened back in 1870, this
is the place to go for *cocido
madrileño* (soup followed by
chickpeas and a selection
of meats) cooked in the
traditional way over a wood
fire. Try the delicious *buñuelos
de manzana* (battered apples)
for pudding, and don't plan
on doing anything energetic
afterwards. Around €30 a head,
but they don't accept cards.

LA BOLA

EL BUEY

Plaza de la Marina Española 1
Ⓜ Santo Domingo or Ópera ☏ 915 413
041. Mon–Sat 1–4pm & 9pm–midnight, Sun
1–4pm. MAP P.40, POCKET MAP C4

A meat-eaters' paradise,
specializing in superb steak
that you fry yourself on a
hotplate. Great side dishes and
home-made desserts, with a
highly drinkable house red, all
for around €35 per head.

CASA GALLEGA

C/Bordadores 11 Ⓜ Ópera or Sol
☏ 915 419 055; also Plaza San Miguel 8
Ⓜ Ópera or Sol ☏ 915 473 055. Both daily
noon–midnight. MAP P.40, POCKET MAP C11

Two airy and welcoming
marisquerías that have been
importing seafood on overnight
trains from Galicia since
opening in 1915. Costs vary
according to the market price
of the fish or shellfish that you
order. *Pulpo* (octopus) and
pimientos de Padrón (small
peppers, spiced up by the odd
fiery one) are brilliantly done
and relatively inexpensive,
but the more exotic seasonal
delights will raise a bill to
around €50 a head.

ENTRE SUSPIRO Y SUSPIRO

C/Caños de Peral 3 Ⓜ Ópera ☏ 915 420 644.
Mon–Fri 2–5pm & 9–1am, Sat 9–1am.
MAP P.40, POCKET MAP B10

Given Madrid's links with
Latin America, this is one
of surprisingly few decent
Mexican restaurants in the
city. Quesadillas, tacos and
some imaginative takes on
traditional dishes served up
in pleasant surroundings,
although it is rather cramped
and prices are high at around
€40 for a meal.

EL ESCARPÍN

C/Hileras 17 Ⓜ Ópera ☏ 915 599 957. Daily
9am–4.30pm & 8pm–midnight. MAP P.40,
POCKET MAP C11

Reasonably-priced Asturian
bar-restaurant offering regional
specialities including *chorizo
a la sidra* (chorizo with cider),
alubias con almejas (beans with
clams) and, of course, cider.
Eat tapas at the bar or try the
brick-lined dining room.

Bars

EL ANCIANO REY DE LOS VINOS

C/Bailén 19 Ⓜ Ópera. Mon, Tues & Thurs–Sun
10am–3pm & 6–11pm. MAP P.40, POCKET MAP C6

Traditional standing-room-
only bar founded back in 1909,
serving well-poured beer,
vermút, a decent selection of
wine and some good tapas.

Club

JOY MADRID

C/Arenal 11 Ⓜ Sol or Ópera Ⓦ www.joy
-eslava.com. Daily midnight–6am. €10–15
including first drink. MAP P.40, POCKET MAP C11

This long-standing club is one
of the staples of the Madrid
night scene. It has a busy
schedule of sessions every
day of the week, catering for
everything from house to 70's
disco. If you arrive early there
are discounts on the entry fee.

Live music

CAFÉ DE CHINITAS

C/Torija 7 Ⓜ Santo Domingo ☏ 915 595 135,
Ⓦ www.chinitas.com. Mon–Thurs 9pm–2am,
Fri & Sat 9pm–3am. Drinks and show €32.
MAP P.40, POCKET MAP C4

One of the oldest flamenco
clubs in Madrid, hosting a
dinner-dance spectacular. The
music is authentic but keep an
eye on how much you order
as the bill can mount up very
quickly indeed. Be sure to
make an advance reservation.

LA COQUETTE

C/Hileras 14 Ⓜ Ópera. Mon–Sat
8pm–2.30am. Closed Aug. MAP P.40, POCKET
MAP C11

A small, crowded basement
jazz and blues bar, where
people sit around watching the
band perform on a tiny stage.
Midweek is the best bet if you
want to try and get a seat,
whilst weekends can get very
packed.

JOY

Rastro, Lavapiés and Embajadores

Lavapiés and Embajadores were originally tough, working-class districts built to accommodate the huge population growth of Madrid in the eighteenth and nineteenth centuries. Traditional sights are thin on the ground, but some original tenement blocks survive and the area is now famous for the Rastro street market. These barrios are also home to the *castizos* – authentic Madrileños – who can be seen decked out in traditional costume during local festivals. The character of these areas has changed, however, in recent years. Young Spaniards and large numbers of immigrants have arrived, meaning that Lavapiés and Embajadores are now Madrid's most racially mixed barrios, with teahouses, kebab joints and textile shops sitting alongside some of the most original bars and restaurants in the city. Petty crime can be a problem round here but the reality is not as dramatic as newspapers suggest.

IGLESIA COLEGIATA DE SAN ISIDRO

C/Toledo 37 🚇 Tirso de Molina or La Latina. Mon–Sat 7.45am–1pm & 6–8.45pm, Sun & hols 8.30am–2pm & 6–8.30pm. MAP P.48–49, POCKET MAP C14

Built from 1622 to 1633, this enormous twin-towered church was originally the centre of the Jesuit Order in Spain. After Carlos III fell out with the Order in 1767, he redesigned the interior and dedicated it to the city's patron, San Isidro. Isidro's remains – and those of his equally saintly wife – were brought here in 1769 from the nearby **Iglesia de San Andrés** (see p.33). The church was the city's cathedral from 1886 until 1993 when the **Catedral de la Almudena** (see p.39) was completed. It has a single nave with ornate lateral chapels and an impressive altarpiece.

MERCADO DEL RASTRO

🚇 La Latina. MAP P.48–49, POCKET MAP D8

Every Sunday morning the heaving, ramshackle mass of El Rastro fleamarket takes over Calle Ribera de Curtidores. On

SAN CAYETANO

offer is just about anything you might – or more likely might not – need, from old clothes and military surplus to caged birds and fine antiques. Real bargains are rare, but the atmosphere is enjoyable and the nearby bars are as good as any in the city. Petty theft is common, so keep a close eye on your belongings. If you're looking for something more upmarket, try the antiques shops in **Galerías Piquer** at C/Ribera de Curtidores 29, which are also open Sunday mornings.

ESTADIO VICENTE CALDERÓN

Paseo Virgen del Puerto 67 Ⓜ Pirámides
☎ 902 260 403 www.clubatleticodemadrid
.com. Match tickets from €30; ☎ 902 530 500 and via the website. MAP P.48-49, POCKET MAP B1

Home to **Atlético Madrid**, one of the city's two big-name football teams, this 54,000-capacity stadium is quite a sight, with its smoked-glass sides rising high above the Manzanares river. Atlético may not have tasted the glory experienced by rivals Real Madrid, but they still rank as one of Spain's biggest teams. The stadium houses a club shop (Mon–Fri 10am–2pm & 2–8pm, Sat & Sun 10am–2pm, match days 11am–45 mins before kickoff) and a museum (Tues–Sun 11am–7pm; €6; guided tours Tues–Fri 1pm & 5.30pm, Sat & Sun noon, 1pm, 4.30pm & 5.30pm, depending on match times) detailing the club's history and successes.

LA CORRALA

C/Tribulete 12 Ⓜ Lavapiés. MAP P.48-49, POCKET MAP E8

Built in 1839 and restored in the 1980s, this is one of many traditional *corrales* (tenement blocks) in Lavapiés, with balconied apartments opening onto a central patio. Plays, especially farces and *zarzuelas* (a mix of classical opera and music-hall), used to be performed regularly in *corrales*; this one usually hosts summer performances.

SAN CAYETANO

C/Embajadores 15 Ⓜ Tirso de Molina or La Latina. Variable hours, usually Mon–Sat 9.30am–12pm & 6–8pm, Sun 9am–2pm & 6–8pm. MAP P.48-49, POCKET MAP E8

José de Churriguera and Pedro de Ribera, both renowned for their extravagant designs, were involved in the design of the elaborate facade, which dates from 1761. Most of the rest of the church was destroyed in the Civil War and has since been rebuilt.

PLAZA LAVAPIÉS

Ⓜ Lavapiés. MAP P.48-49, POCKET MAP F8

In the Middle Ages, bustling Plaza Lavapiés was the core of Jewish Madrid, with the synagogue situated on the site now occupied by the Teatro Valle-Inclán. Today, with its Chinese, Arabic and African inhabitants, it remains a cosmopolitan place, and the plaza, along with Calle Argumosa running off from its southeastern corner, is an animated spot, with a variety of bars and cafés in various states of decay.

CALLE ATOCHA

Ⓜ Atocha or Antón Martín. MAP P.48-49, POCKET MAP E6-H8

Calle Atocha, one of the old ceremonial routes from Plaza Mayor to the basilica at Atocha, forms the northeastern border of Lavapiés. At its southern end it's a mishmash of fast-food and touristy restaurants, developing, as you move north up the hill, into a strange mixture of cheap hostels, fading shops, bars, lottery kiosks and sex emporia. With its brash neon lighting and shiny black facade, the huge sex shop at no. 80, El Mundo Fantástico, stands unashamedly opposite a convent and the site of an old printing house that produced the first edition of the first part of *Don Quixote*.

CINE DORÉ

C/Santa Isabel 3 Ⓜ Antón Martín
☎ 914 672 600. Closed Mon. Films €2.50.
MAP P.48-49, POCKET MAP F14

At the end of the narrow Pasaje Doré alley is the Cine Doré, the **oldest cinema** in Madrid. Dating from 1922 with a later

Modernista/Art Nouveau facade, it's now the **Filmoteca Nacional**, an art-house cinema with bargain prices and a pleasant, inexpensive café/restaurant (Tues–Sun 4–11pm).

MUSEO DEL FERROCARRIL

Paseo de las Delicias 61 Ⓜ Delicias
☎ 902 228 822 ⓦ www.museodelferrocarril
.org. Tues–Thurs & Sun 10am–3pm, Fri & Sat 10am–8pm. Closed Aug. €5.09, Sat €2.04. MAP P.48–49, POCKET MAP H9

The Museo del Ferrocarril (Railway Museum) contains an impressive assortment of engines, carriages and wagons that once graced the train lines of Spain. The museum, which is housed in the handsome old station of Delicias, also has a fascinating collection of **model railways** and there's an atmospheric little café in one of the more elegant carriages.

CINE DORÉ

CLUB	
El Juglar	2

LIVE MUSIC	
Casa Patas	1

RESTAURANTS	
Asador Arizmendi	3
Casa Lastra Sidrería	4
Gaudeamus Café	12
Malacatín	8
La Sanabresa	2

TAPAS BARS	
Casa Amadeo "Los Caracoles"	6
Cervecería "Los Caracoles"	13
Freiduría de Gallinejas	15
Melo's	9
La Musa Espronceda	7
Taberna de Antonio Sánchez	5

Cafés

LA LIBRE

C/Argumosa 39 Ⓜ Lavapiés. Mon–Thurs 9am–10pm, Fri–Sun 10am–11.30pm. MAP P.48–49, POCKET MAP G8

A café/bookshop nestling behind the Reina Sofía museum where you can sit back in a comfy chair, thumb through one of their second-hand books (some in English) and enjoy brunch, home-made cakes or a snack.

NUEVO CAFÉ BARBIERI

C/Ave María 45 Ⓜ Lavapiés. Mon–Thurs 3pm–12.30am, Fri & Sat 3pm–2.30am, Sun 1pm–12.30am. MAP P.48–49, POCKET MAP F8

A relaxed, slightly dilapidated café, with unobtrusive music, wooden tables, newspapers and a wide selection of coffees.

Restaurants

ASADOR ARIZMENDI

Plaza Tirso de Molina 7, 1° (entrance on C/Jesus y Maria) Ⓜ Tirso de Molina ☎ 914 295 030. Mon–Sat 1–4pm & 9pm–midnight, Sun 1–4pm. MAP P.48–49, POCKET MAP D14

The new ownership has retained this neighbourhood restaurant's charm – it's still the locals' choice for long lunches. There's a range of delicious Castilian dishes and fine home-made desserts. There's a €25 lunchtime special menu; you'll pay €40–45 during the evening.

CASA LASTRA SIDRERÍA

C/Olivar 3 Ⓜ Antón Martín ☎ 913 690 837. Thurs–Tues 1–4pm & 8pm–midnight. Closed July. MAP P.48–49, POCKET MAP E14

Moderately priced Asturian fare: *chorizo a la sidra* (chorizo in cider), *fabada* (a stew of beans, chorizo and black pudding) and, of course, *sidra* (cider).

GAUDEAMUS CAFÉ

Edificio Escuelas Pias, C/Tribulete 14, 4° Ⓜ Lavapiés. ☎ 915 282 594. Mon–Fri 11am–midnight, Sat & hols 1.30pm–midnight, closed Sun. No cards. MAP P.48–49, POCKET MAP E8

Fabulous creative tapas-style dishes such as fried aubergines in rosemary honey and some really tasty chocolate desserts at this rooftop restaurant. It is not easy to find, though; make your way up past the library to the top floor. Menus €12.80 (lunch); €27 (evening).

MALACATÍN

C/Ruda 5 Ⓜ La Latina ☎ 913 655 241. Mon–Sat 11am–5.30pm, Thurs & Fri also open 8.15–11pm. Closed July 13–Aug 21. MAP P.48–49, POCKET MAP D8

Established in 1895 to serve wine to local workmen, this authentic *castizo* restaurant serves generous helpings of arguably the best *cocido* in the city for a reasonable €19.50. Sample it at the bar for €5 too.

LA SANABRESA

C/Amor de Diós 12 Ⓜ Antón Martín ☎ 914 290 338. Mon–Sat 1–4.30pm & 8.30–11.30pm, Fri & Sat till midnight. Closed Aug. MAP P.48–49, POCKET MAP G14

Unpretentious place with reasonably priced dishes. There are two *menús del día* for around €10 and a weekend set lunch for €12. Don't miss the grilled aubergines.

Tapas bars

CASA AMADEO "LOS CARACOLES"

Plaza Cascorro 18 Ⓜ La Latina. Mon–Thurs 11am–4pm, Fri & Sat 11am–4pm & 7–10.30pm, Sun 10am–4pm. MAP P.48–49, POCKET MAP D7

A favourite since the 1940s, with tapas ranging from the eponymous *caracoles* (snails), *callos* and *oreja*. It's heaving on Sundays after the market.

CERVECERÍA "LOS CARACOLES"

C/Toledo 106 ⓂPuerta de Toledo. Tues–Sat 9am–10.30pm, Sun 9am–4pm. Closed July. MAP P.48–49, POCKET MAP C8

Rough-and-ready bar specializing in snails, washed down with local *vermút del grifo* (draught vermouth).

FREIDURIA DE GALLINEJAS

C/Embajadores 84 Ⓜ Embajadores. Mon–Sat 11am–11pm. Closed Aug. MAP P.48–49, POCKET MAP F9

This traditional tiled, family-run bar is famed for serving the best fried lambs' intestines in the city. A variety of different cuts are available as well as straightforward fried lamb.

MELO'S

C/Ave María 44 Ⓜ Lavapiés. Tues–Sat 9am–2am. Closed Aug. MAP P.48–49, POCKET MAP F8

Standing room only at this very popular Galician bar serving huge *zapatillas* (bread filled with *lacón* – shoulder of pork – and cheese) plus great *pimientos de Padrón*.

LA MUSA ESPRONCEDA

C/Santa Isabel 17 Ⓜ Atocha or Antón Martín. Daily 1.30–4pm & 8pm–midnight. MAP P.48–49, POCKET MAP G7

Great value tapas – classics such as tortilla and *croquetas* and creative bites such as brie wrapped in bacon – served in this friendly Lavapiés local. Offers a €10 lunchtime menu.

TABERNA DE ANTONIO SÁNCHEZ

C/Mesón de Paredes 13 ⓂTirso de Molina. Mon–Sat noon–4pm & 8pm–midnight, Sun noon–4.30pm. MAP P.48–49, POCKET MAP E7

Said to be Madrid's oldest *taberna*, this seventeenth-century bar has a stuffed bull's head (in honour of Antonio Sánchez, the founder's son, who was killed by one) and a wooden interior.

Lots of *finos*, plus *jamón* tapas or *tortilla de San Isidro* (salt cod omelette).

Bars

ICE BAR

C/Conde de Romanones 3 ⓂTirso de Molina. Daily 5–11pm, Fri & Sat till 2am. Closed Aug. MAP P.48–49, POCKET MAP D13

The coldest if not the coolest bar in the city. For €15 (coat and cocktail included) you will be transported to a polar world complete with frozen furniture.

LA INQUILINA

C/Ave María 39 Ⓜ Lavapiés. Tues–Thurs 7pm–2am, Fri–Sun 1–4pm & 8pm–3am. MAP P.48–49, POCKET MAP F8

Once an old furniture shop, now a mainstay on the Lavapiés bar scene, *La Inquilina* is a deceptively large, bohemian bar that hosts regular art exhibitions and acoustic concerts.

Club

EL JUGLAR

C/Lavapiés 37 Ⓜ Lavapiés Ⓦ www.salajuglar .com. Wed–Sun 9.30pm–3am, Fri & Sat till 3.30am. MAP P.48–49, POCKET MAP F8

Down-to-earth club with DJs playing funk and soul. There are also regular concerts with an entry fee of around €10.

Live music

CASA PATAS

C/Cañizares 10 ⓂAntón Martín or Tirso Molina ☎913 690 496 Ⓦwww.casapatas.com. Shows: Mon–Thurs 10.30pm, Fri & Sat 9pm & midnight. €25–30. MAP P.48–49, POCKET MAP E14

Authentic flamenco club with a bar and restaurant that gets its share of big names. The best nights are Thursday and Friday – check website for schedules.

4

Sol, Santa Ana and Huertas

The busy streets around Puerta del Sol, Plaza Santa Ana and Huertas are the bustling heart of Madrid and the reference point for most visitors to the capital. The city began to expand here during the sixteenth century and the area subsequently became known as the *barrio de las letras* (literary neighbourhood) because of the many authors and playwrights – including Cervantes – who made it their home. Today, the literary theme continues, with theatres, bookshops and cafés proliferating alongside the Círculo de Bellas Artes (Fine Arts Institute), the Teatro Español (historic theatre specializing in classic works) and the Congreso de Los Diputados (Parliament). For art lovers, there's the Real Academia de Bellas Artes de San Fernando museum, but for most visitors, though, the main attraction is the vast array of traditional bars, particularly concentrated around the picturesque Plaza Santa Ana.

PUERTA DEL SOL

Ⓜ Sol. MAP P.54, POCKET MAP D11

This half-moon-shaped plaza, thronged with people at almost any hour of the day, marks the epicentre of Madrid and, indeed, of Spain – **Kilometre Zero**, an inconspicuous stone slab on the south side of the square, is the spot from which all distances in the country are measured. Opposite is an equestrian bronze of King Carlos III, and to the east a statue of Madrid's emblem, *el oso y el madroño* (bear and strawberry tree).

The square has been a popular meeting place since the mid-sixteenth century, when it was the site of one of the main gates into the city. Its most important building is the Casa de Correos, built in 1766 and originally the city's post office. Under Franco it became the headquarters of the much-feared security police and it now houses the main offices of the Madrid regional government. The neoclassical facade is crowned by the nation's most famous clock which officially ushers in the New Year: on December 31, Madrileños pack Puerta del Sol and attempt to scoff twelve grapes – one on each of the chimes of midnight – to bring themselves good luck for the next twelve months.

The square has also witnessed several incidents of national importance, including the slaughter of a rioting crowd by Napoleon's marshal, Murat, aided by the infamous Egyptian cavalry, on May 2, 1808. The massacre is depicted in Goya's canvas, *Dos de Mayo*, now hanging in the Prado (see p.66).

PLAZA SANTA ANA

Ⓜ Sol or Antón Martín. MAP P.54, POCKET MAP F13

The main reason for visiting vibrant Plaza Santa Ana is the mass of bars, restaurants and cafés on the square itself and in the nearby streets that bring the area alive in the evenings.

The square was one of a series created by Joseph Bonaparte, whose passion for open spaces led to a remarkable remodelling of Madrid in the six short years of his reign. It's dominated by two distinguished buildings at either end: to the west, the *ME Madrid Reina Victoria*, a giant white confection of a hotel; to the east, the nineteenth-century Neoclassical Teatro Español. There has been a playhouse on this site since 1583, and the current theatre is the oldest in Madrid, its facade decorated

PLAZA SANTA ANA

with busts of famous Spanish playwrights.

CASA DE LOPE DE VEGA

C/Cervantes 11 Ⓜ Antón Martín. Tues–Sat 10am–3pm. Closed mid-July to mid-Aug. Free guided tours; wait for a group to be formed; ring 914 299 216 to reserve a tour in English. MAP P.54, POCKET MAP G13

Situated in the heart of the Huertas district, the reconstructed home of the great Golden Age Spanish dramatist offers a fascinating glimpse of life in seventeenth-century Madrid. Lope de Vega, a prolific writer with a tangled private life, lived here for 25 years until his death in 1635 at the age of 72. The house itself has been furnished in authentic fashion using the inventory left at the writer's death and highlights include a chapel containing some of his relics, his study with a selection of contemporary books, an Arabic-style drawing room and a delightful courtyard garden.

Cervantes lived and died at no. 2 on the same street and though the original building has long gone, a plaque above a shop marks the site.

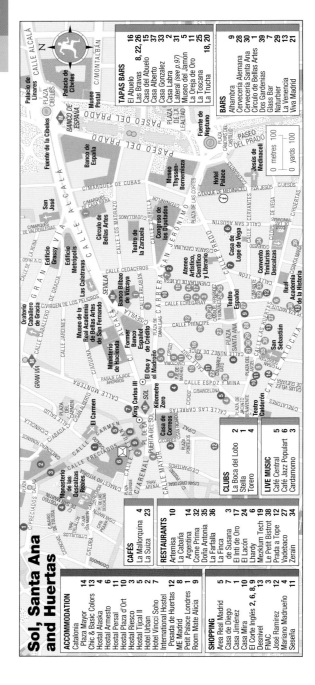

Sol, Santa Ana and Huertas

ACCOMMODATION

Catalonia	
Plaza Mayor	14
Chic & Basic Colors	13
Hostal Alaska	4
Hostal Armesto	6
Hostal Persal	11
Hostal Plaza d'Ort	10
Hostal Riesco	3
Hostal Tijcal II	5
Hotel Urban	2
Hotel Vincci Soho	7
International Hostel	
Posada de Huertas	12
ME Madrid	8
Petit Palace Londres	1
Room Mate Alicia	9

SHOPPING

Area Real Madrid	5
Casa de Diego	7
Casa Jiménez	10
Casa Mira	4
El Corte Inglés	2, 6, 8, 9
Desnivel	13
FNAC	1
José Ramírez	12
Mariano Madrueño	4
Seseña	11

CAFÉS

La Mallorquina	4
La Suiza	23

RESTAURANTS

Artemisa	10
La Cabaña	
Argentina	14
Come Prima	32
Doña Antonia	35
La Farfalla	36
La Finca	
de Susana	3
El Inti de Oro	17
El Lacón	24
Lhardy	6
Mezklum Tech	19
Le Petit Bistrot	38
Prada a Tope	12
Vadebaco	27
Zerain	34

CLUBS

La Boca del Lobo	2
Stella	1
Torero	4

LIVE MUSIC

Café Central	5
Café Jazz Populart	6
Cardamomo	3

TAPAS BARS

El Abuelo	16
Las Bravas	8, 22, 26
Casa del Abuelo	15
Casa Alberto	37
Casa Gonzalez	33
Casa Labra	2
Lateral (see p.97)	31
Museo del Jamón	5
La Oreja de Oro	11
La Toscana	25
La Trucha	18, 20

BARS

Alhambra	9
Cervecería Alemana	28
Cervecería Santa Ana	30
Círculo de Bellas Artes	1
Dos Gardenias	39
Glass Bar	7
Naturbier	29
La Venencia	13
Viva Madrid	21

54

ATENEO ARTÍSTICO, CIENTÍFICO Y LITERARIO

C/Prado 2 Ⓜ Antón Martín or Sevilla.
MAP P.54, POCKET MAP G12

The Ateneo (literary, scientific and political club) was founded after the 1820 Revolution and provided a focus for the new liberal political ideas circulating at that time. The exterior is neo-Plateresque in style, while the inside features a neoclassical lecture theatre, a wooden panelled corridor with portraits of past presidents of the club and a splendid reading room. It also has a café and hosts occasional exhibitions.

CONGRESO DE LOS DIPUTADOS

Plaza de las Cortes Ⓜ Sevilla Ⓦ www
.congreso.es. Sat 10.30am–12.30pm
(bring passport). Closed Aug & hols.
MAP P.54, POCKET MAP G12

The lower house of the **Spanish parliament** meets in a rather unprepossessing nineteenth-century building; its most distinguished feature is the two bronze lions that guard the entrance, made from a melted-down cannon captured during the African War of 1859–60. Sessions can be visited by appointment only, though you can turn up and queue for a free tour on Saturday mornings. This takes in several important rooms and the chamber with the bullet holes left by mad Colonel Tejero and his Guardia Civil associates in the abortive coup of 1981.

CALLE ALCALÁ

Ⓜ Sol or Sevilla. MAP P.54, POCKET MAP E11–J10

An imposing catalogue of Spanish architecture lines Calle Alcalá, an ancient thoroughfare that originally led to the university town of Alcalá de Henares. It starts at Puerta del Sol and in this first stretch look out parti-cularly for the splendid early twentieth-century wedge-shaped Banco Español de Crédito adorned with **elephant heads** and plaques listing all the branches of the bank in Spain, soon to be turned into a luxury hotel, shopping centre and apartment block. The Banco de Bilbao Vizcaya, with its neoclassical facade complete with charioteers on top, and the baroque Ministerio de Hacienda (Inland Revenue) are similarly impressive.

IGLESIA DE SAN JOSÉ

C/Alcalá 41 Ⓜ Banco de España. Daily 7am–12.30pm & 6–8.30pm, Sun open from 9am. MAP P.54, POCKET MAP G10

The red-brick Iglesia de San José, near the junction with Gran Vía, dates back to the 1730s and was the last building designed by the prolific Pedro de Ribera. The interior holds the ornate Santa Teresa de Ávila chapel and an impressive collection of colourful images of Christ and the Virgin Mary.

IGLESIA DE LAS CALATRAVAS

C/Alcalá 25 Ⓜ Sevilla. Mon–Fri 8am–1pm & 6–8pm, Sat & Sun 11am–2pm & 6–8pm. MAP P.54, POCKET MAP F11

The pastel-pink Iglesia de las Calatravas was built in the seventeenth century for the nuns of the Calatrava, one of the four Spanish military orders. Inside, it contains a fantastically elaborate gold altarpiece by José Churriguera.

MUSEO DE LA REAL ACADEMIA DE BELLAS ARTES DE SAN FERNANDO

C/Alcalá 13 Ⓜ Sevilla ☎ 915 240 864 ⓦ realacademiabellasartessanfernando.com. Tues–Sun 10am–3pm. €5, free Wed. MAP P.54, POCKET MAP F11

Established by Felipe V in 1744 and housed in its present location since 1773, the Museo de la Real Academia de Bellas Artes de San Fernando is one of the most important art galleries in Spain. Its displays include sections on sculpture, architecture and music, some interesting French and Italian work and an extraordinary – but chaotically displayed – collection of Spanish paintings, including El Greco, Velázquez, Murillo and Picasso.

The Goya section has two revealing self-portraits, several depictions of the despised royal favourite *Don Manuel Godoy*, the desolate representation of *The Madhouse* and *The Burial of the Sardine* (a popular procession that continues to this day in Madrid).

The gallery also holds the national copper engraving collection (Mon–Thurs 9am–5pm, Fri 9am–3pm; free), which includes Goya etchings and several of the copper plates used for his *Capricho* series on show in the Prado.

CÍRCULO DE BELLAS ARTES

C/Marqués de Casa Riera 2 Ⓜ Banco de España. Exhibitions Tues–Sat 11am–2pm & 5–9pm, Sun 11am–2pm. €3. MAP P.54, POCKET MAP G11

This striking 1920s Art Deco

building, crowned by a statue of Pallas Athene, is home to one of Madrid's best arts centres. Inside there's a theatre, music hall, galleries, cinema and café bar (see p.64). For many years a stronghold of Spain's intelligentsia, it attracts the city's arts and media crowd but is not exclusive, nor expensive. As the Círculo is theoretically a members-only club, it issues day membership on the door.

PLAZA DE CIBELES

Ⓜ Banco de España. MAP P.54, POCKET MAP J10
Encircled by four of the most monumental buildings in Madrid, Plaza de Cibeles is one of the city's most famous landmarks. At its centre, and marooned in a sea of never-ending traffic, is the late eighteenth-century fountain and statue of the goddess Cybele riding in a lion-drawn chariot. Built to celebrate the city's first public water supply, today the fountain is the post-victory congregation point for Real Madrid fans (Atlético supporters bathe in the fountain of Neptune just down the road).

PALACIO DE CIBELES

Ⓜ Banco de España Ⓦ centrocentro.org.
Exhibitions Tues–Sun 10am–8pm. MAP P.54,
POCKET MAP J10
This grandiose wedding-cake of a building on the eastern side of Paseo del Prado, constructed between 1904 and 1917 by the prolific architect partnership of Antonio Palacios and Joaquín Otamendi, was once Madrid's main post office, but has recently been usurped by the Madrid City Council. It is now home to a smart new exhibition space, a viewing gallery (Tues–Sun 10.30am–1.30pm & 4–7pm; €2, under-12s €0.50), a café (daily

PALACIO DE CIBELES

10am–midnight), expensive restaurant (daily 1.30–4.30pm & 8pm–midnight) run by Toledan restaurateur Adolfo Muñoz, and an overpriced and rather *pijo* terrace bar (daily 10am–2am), which does offer some great views over the Paseo del Prado.

PALACIO DE LINARES

Plaza de Cibeles 2 Ⓜ Banco de España
Ⓦ www.casamerica.es. Exhibitions usually
Mon–Sat 11am–8pm, Sun 11am–3pm;
guided tours Sat & Sun 11am, noon, 1pm. €8,
students and over-65s €5, under-12s free.
Closed Aug. MAP P.54, POCKET MAP J10
This palatial eighteenth-century mansion, built by the Marqués de Linares, is now home to the Casa de América, a cultural organization that promotes Latin American art through concerts, films and exhibitions. At weekends there are guided tours through the sumptuous mansion decorated with some marvellous frescoes, crystal chandeliers and elaborate tapestries from the Real Fábrica (see p.76). The palacio also has an expensive designer restaurant and an excellent summer garden terrace.

Shops

AREA REAL MADRID

C/Carmen 3 ⓂSol. Mon–Sat 10am–9pm,
Sun 11am–8pm. MAP P.54, POCKET MAP D11

Club store where you can pick
up replica shirts and all manner
of – expensive – souvenirs
related to the club's history.
There is another branch (see
p.95) in the shopping centre on
the corner of Real's Bernabéu
stadium at C/Concha Espina 1.

CASA DE DIEGO

Puerta del Sol 12 ⓂSol. Mon–Sat
9.30am–8pm. MAP P.54, POCKET MAP E11

Old-fashioned shop with
helpful staff selling a fabulous
array of Spanish fans (*abanicos*)
ranging from cheap offerings at
under €10 to beautifully handcrafted works of art costing
up to €200. Sells umbrellas,
walking sticks and shawls too.

CASA JIMÉNEZ

C/Preciados 42 ⓂCallao. Mon–Sat
10am–1.30pm & 5–8pm, closed Sat pm in July
and all day Sat in Aug. MAP P.54, POCKET MAP C10

Traditional establishment that
has changed little since it first
opened its doors back in 1923.
Casa Jiménez is renowned for
its elaborately embroidered
mantones (shawls) made in
Seville (prices range from €100

to €600), as well as its gorgeous
fans starting at around €40.

CASA MIRA

Carrera de San Jerónimo 30 ⓂSevilla. Daily
10am–2pm & 5–9pm. MAP P.54, POCKET MAP F12

The place to go for *turrón*
(flavoured nougat, eaten by
Spaniards at Christmas) and
marzipan. The family business
has been open for over a
150 years since the founder,
Luis Mira, arrived from
Asturias and set up a stall in
Puerta del Sol.

EL CORTE INGLÉS

C/Preciados 1–4 ⓂSol & Plaza Callao 2
ⓂCallao. Mon–Sat 10am–9pm & first Sun in
the month. MAP P.54, POCKET MAP D10–D11

The Spanish department store
par excellence. It's not cheap,
but the quality is very good, the
staff are highly professional (the
majority speak English) and
there's a gourmet section on the
ninth floor of the Callao branch
with fantastic views over the
city (see p.88).

DESNIVEL

Plaza Matute 6 ⓂAntón Martín. Mon–Sat
10am–2pm & 4.30–8.30pm. MAP P.54, POCKET
MAP F14

A great selection of maps and
guides if you fancy a hike in
the nearby Sierra Guadarrama.

CASA DE DIEGO

FNAC

C/Preciados 28 Ⓜ Callao. Mon–Sat
10am–9.30pm, Sun noon–9.30pm. MAP P.54,
POCKET MAP D10

French department store with
sections for books, videos, CDs
and electrical equipment. Also
sells concert tickets.

JOSÉ RAMÍREZ

C/Paz 8 Ⓜ Sol. Mon–Fri 10am–2pm & 5–8pm,
Sat 10am–2pm. MAP P.54, POCKET MAP D12

The Ramírez family have been
making handcrafted guitars
since 1882 and, even if you are
not a budding flamenco artist,
this beautiful old shop is still
worth a visit to appreciate these
works of art used by some of
the world's leading musicians.

MARIANO MADRUEÑO

C/Postigo San Martín 3 Ⓜ Callao. Mon–Fri
9.30am–2pm & 5–8pm, Sat 9.30am–2pm.
MAP P.54, POCKET MAP C10

Traditional wine seller's, established in 1895, where there's an
overpowering smell of grapes
as you peruse its vintage-
crammed shelves. Intriguing
tipples include potent Licor
de Hierbas from Galicia and
home-made Pacharán (aniseed
liqueur with sloe berries).

SESEÑA

C/Cruz 23 Ⓜ Sol. Mon–Sat 10am–1.30pm &
4.30–8pm. MAP P.54, POCKET MAP E12

Open since 1901, this shop
specializes in traditional
Madrileño capes for royalty
and celebrities. Clients have
included Luis Buñuel, Gary
Cooper and Hillary Clinton.

Cafés

LA MALLORQUINA

Puerta del Sol 2 Ⓜ Sol. Daily 9am–9.15pm.
MAP P.54, POCKET MAP D12

Classic Madrid café, great for
breakfast or sweet snacks.

SESEÑA

Try one of their *napolitanas*
(cream slices) in the upstairs
salon that overlooks Puerta
del Sol.

LA SUIZA

Plaza Santa Ana 2 Ⓜ Antón Martín or
Sevilla. Daily 7am–midnight. MAP P.54,
POCKET MAP F13

A traditional Madrid café
serving delicious *leche
merengada* (a sort of sweet
whipped-milk ice cream) and a
bewildering array of cakes.

Restaurants

ARTEMISA

C/Ventura de la Vega 4 Ⓜ Sevilla
☎ 914 295 092. Daily 1.30–4pm &
9pm–midnight. MAP P.54, POCKET MAP F12

Long-standing vegetarian
restaurant, serving a wide range
of dishes including nettle soup
and some delicious aubergine
croquetas. For the indecisive
there are sampler menus for
two at around €25.

LA CABAÑA ARGENTINA

C/Ventura de la Vega 10 Ⓜ Sevilla
☎ 913 697 202. Daily 1pm–midnight, Fri & Sat
until 12.30am. MAP P.54, POCKET MAP F12

One of the best Argentine
eateries in the city. Excellent-
quality meat (*el bife lomo alto*
is a house favourite) and
classic desserts including
panqueques. Friendly service
and only around €35 a head.

COME PRIMA

C/Echegaray 27 ⓜ Antón Martín
☎ 914 203 042. Mon 9pm–midnight, Tues-Sat 1.30–4pm & 9pm–midnight. Closed Aug.
MAP P.54, POCKET MAP F13

Superior Italian restaurant, with fresh ingredients, excellent antipasti and authentic main courses including a great seafood risotto. Very popular, so make sure you book, and expect to pay around €35 a head.

DOÑA ANTONIA

C/ Huertas 4 ⓜ Antón Martín/Sol
☎ 911 568 208. Tues–Sun 1.30pm–midnight.
MAP P.54, POCKET MAP E13

Original tapas-style dishes such as chicken teriyaki and fried vegetables with rosemary oil as well as more traditional home cooking at this all-day restaurant in Huertas. Tea is served up in the afternoon together with some mouth-watering chocolate tart and cheesecake. Open till 2am at weekends.

LA FARFALLA

C/Huertas 6 ⓜ Antón Martín ☎ 913 694 391.
Mon–Thurs 1–4.30pm & 8.30pm–2.30am, Fri-Sun 1pm–2.30am. MAP P.54, POCKET MAP E13

Deservedly popular Italian-Argentine restaurant that is one of the stalwarts of the Huertas scene. There's a fantastic selection of pizzas (around €7–8) and Argentine meats (the €18.75 *parrillada* serves two), plus some very appetising home-made desserts. As well as being good value, it is also open especially late: a good option if you suffer from late-night hunger pangs.

LA FINCA DE SUSANA

C/Arlabán 4 ⓜ Sevilla. Daily 1–3.45pm & 8.30–11.45pm. MAP P.54, POCKET MAP F11

One of three great-value restaurants set up by a group of Catalan friends (another, *La Gloria de Montera* is just off Gran Vía, see p.87). A varied *menú del día* for around €10 consists of simple dishes cooked with imagination. Efficient, but impersonal service. Arrive early to avoid queuing, as you can't book.

EL INTI DE ORO

C/Ventura de la Vega 12 ⓜ Antón Martín
☎ 914 296 703. Daily 1.30–4pm & 8.30pm–midnight. Also at c/Amor de Dios 9 ⓜ Antón Martín ☎ 914 291 958. MAP P.54, POCKET MAP F12

The friendly staff at this good-value Peruvian restaurant are more than ready to provide suggestions for those new to the cuisine. The pisco sour, a cocktail of Peruvian liquor, lemon juice, egg white and sugar is a recommended starter, while the *cebiche de merluza* (raw fish marinated in lemon juice) is a wonderful dish. A full meal costs around €30.

EL LACÓN

C/Manuel Fernández y González 8 ⓜ Sol
☎ 914 296 042. Daily 1–4pm, 8pm–midnight. Closed Aug. MAP P.54, POCKET MAP F12

A large Galician bar-restaurant with plenty of seats upstairs. Great *pulpo*, *caldo gallego* (meat and vegetable broth)

MEENKUM TECH

and empanadas. They also do a neat *menú exprés* at lunchtime consisting of a single course and a drink for just €4.

LHARDY

Carrera de San Jerónimo 8 Ⓜ Sol
☎ 915 213 385. Restaurant: Mon–Sat 1–3.30pm & 9–11.30pm, Sun 1–3.30pm. Shop: Mon–Sat 8am–3pm & 5–9.30pm, Sun 9am–2.30pm. Closed Aug. MAP P.54, POCKET MAP E12

Once the haunt of royalty, this is one of Madrid's most beautiful and famous restaurants. It's greatly overpriced – expect to pay over €60 per head for a three-course meal – but on the ground floor, there's a wonderful bar/shop where you can have breakfast or snack on canapés, *fino* and consommé, without breaking the bank.

MEZKLUM TECH

C/Príncipe 16 Ⓜ Sevilla ☎ 915 218 911.
Mon–Thurs 1.30–4pm & 9pm–12.30am, Fri & Sat 1.30–4.30pm & 9pm–1am, Sun 1.30–4.30pm. MAP P.54, POCKET MAP F12

A self-consciously cool and chic arrival on the Santa Ana scene, *Mezklum* is decked out in minimalist style with white, pink and lilac tones and serves a fine array of Mediterranean dishes with good salads and pasta. It has a lunchtime menu at €10.70 and two evening menus at €20 and €25.

LE PETIT BISTROT

Plaza Matute 5 Ⓜ Antón Martín
☎ 914 296 265. Tues–Sat 1.15–3.45pm & 9.15–11.45pm, Sun 11.30–2.30pm. MAP P.54, POCKET MAP F14

A genuine French bistro in a quiet plaza just off Huertas. There's a good set lunch for €13.50 and a hefty Sunday brunch (€18.50). Classics such as onion soup, steak in béarnaise sauce and profiteroles dripping in chocolate are all on offer.

LE PETIT BISTROT

PRADA A TOPE

C/Príncipe 11 Ⓜ Sol ☎ 914 295 921.
Tues–Sun 12.30–5pm & 8pm–midnight. MAP P.54, POCKET MAP F12

Quality produce from the El Bierzo region of León. The *morcilla* (black pudding), *empanada* (pasty) and tortilla are extremely tasty, while the smooth house wines provide the ideal accompaniment.

VADEBACO

C/Prado 4 Ⓜ Sevilla/Antón Martín. Mon–Sat 12.30pm–2am, Sun 12.30–4pm. MAP P.54, POCKET MAP F13

Creative tapas and a vast range of wines at this new arrival just off Plaza Santa Ana. The octopus with spicy potatoes and mushroom risotto are recommended. Cocktail bar and a €12 lunchtime menu too.

ZERAIN

C/Quevedo 3 Ⓜ Antón Martín ☎ 914 297 909.
Mon–Sat 1.30–4pm & 8.30pm–midnight. Closed Aug. MAP P.54, POCKET MAP G13

Basque cider house serving excellent meat and fish dishes. The *chuletón* (T-bone steak) is the speciality, but it also does a very good *tortilla de bacalao* and grilled *rape* (monkfish). Three courses are around €40.

Tapas bars

EL ABUELO

C/Núñez de Arce 5 Ⓜ Sol. Wed–Sun 11.30am–3.30pm & 6.30–11.30pm. MAP P.54, POCKET MAP E12

There's a *comedor* (dining room) at the back of this inexpensive bar, where you can order a selection of traditional *raciones* – the *croquetas* are great – and a jug of house wine.

LAS BRAVAS

C/Alvarez Gato 3 Ⓜ Sol. Other branches at C/Espoz y Mina 13 Ⓜ Sol; & Pasaje Mathéu 5 Ⓜ Sol. Daily noon–4pm & 7pm–midnight. MAP P.54, POCKET MAP E13

Standing room only at these three bars, where, as the name suggests, *patatas bravas* are the thing – they patented their own version of the spicy sauce.

CASA DEL ABUELO

C/Victoria 12 Ⓜ Sol. Daily 11.30am–3.30pm & 6.30–11.30pm. MAP P.54, POCKET MAP E12

A tiny, atmospheric bar serving just their own cloyingly sweet red wine (stick with a beer instead) and delicious cooked prawns – try them *al ajillo* (in garlic) or *a la plancha* (fried) – which are fried up in the tiny corner kitchen.

CASA ALBERTO

C/Huertas 18 Ⓜ Antón Martín
☎ 914 299 356. Tues–Sat noon–1.30am, Sun noon–4pm (in summer). MAP P.54, POCKET MAP F13

Traditional *tasca* that has resisted the passage of time since it was founded back in 1827. Good *caracoles* (snails), *gambas* (prawns) and great *croquetas*, ideally accompanied by a glass of house vermouth.

CASA GONZÁLEZ

C/León 12 Ⓜ Antón Martín. Winter: Tues–Thurs 9am–midnight, Fri & Sat 9am–1am; summer Tues–Sat 5pm–1am. MAP P.54, POCKET MAP F13

Friendly delicatessen/tapas bar with an extensive range of wines and cheese and serving up some great tapas including a fantastic salmorejo, speciality sausage from around Spain and some imaginative tostas covered in a variety of patés.

CASA LABRA

C/Tetuán 12 Ⓜ Sol ☎ 915 310 081. Mon–Sat 11am–3.30pm & 5.30–11pm. MAP P.54, POCKET MAP D11

Dating from 1869 – and where the Spanish Socialist Party was founded ten years later – this traditional and highly popular place (be prepared to queue)

CASA ALBERTO

retains much of its original interior. Order a drink at the bar and a *ración* of *bacalao* (cod fried in batter) or some of the best *croquetas* in town. There's also a restaurant at the back serving classic Madrileño food.

MUSEO DEL JAMÓN

Carrera de San Jerónimo 6 Ⓜ Sol. Mon–Sat 9am–midnight, Sun 10am–midnight. MAP P.54, POCKET MAP E12

This is the largest branch of this unpretentious Madrid chain, from whose ceilings are suspended hundreds of *jamones* (hams). The best – and they're not cheap – are the *jabugos* from the Sierra Morena, though a filling ham sandwich is only around €2.

LA OREJA DE ORO

C/Victoria 9 Ⓜ Sol. May–July & Sept Mon–Sat 1–4pm & 8pm–1am; Oct–April Tues–Sun 1–4pm & 8pm–1am. Closed Aug. MAP P.54, POCKET MAP E12

Standing room only in this spit-and-sawdust bar. Try the excellent *pulpo a la Gallega* (sliced octopus served on a bed of potatoes seasoned with cayenne pepper) washed down with Ribeiro wine. Plenty of other seafood tapas on offer and of course the house speciality *oreja* (pigs' ears) in a spicy sauce.

LA TOSCANA

C/Manuel Fernández y González 10 Ⓜ Antón Martín or Sevilla. Tues–Sat 1–4pm & 8pm–midnight. Closed Aug. MAP P.54, POCKET MAP F12

Home-made tapas in this popular and friendly Huertas classic. The *morcillo* (beef shank) is excellent, while the *croquetas*, *chistorra* and tuna salads are also very tasty.

LA TRUCHA

C/Manuel Fernández y González 3 Ⓜ Antón Martín or Sevilla. ☎ 914 295 833. Branch at C/Nuñez de Arce 6 Ⓜ Sol ☎ 915 320 890. Mon–Sat 12.30–4pm & 7.30pm–midnight. Closed Sun. MAP P.54, POCKET MAP F12

Popular, tourist-oriented tapas bar cum moderately priced restaurant, where delicious smoked fish and *pimientos de Padrón* are the specialities.

Bars

ALHAMBRA

C/Victoria 9 Ⓜ Sol. Daily 11am–1.30am (2am at weekends). MAP P.54, POCKET MAP E12

A friendly tapas bar by day, *Alhambra* transforms itself into a fun disco bar by night with the crowds spilling over into the *El Buscón* bar next door. (draught beer) and go easy on the tapas, as the bill can mount up fast.

CERVECERÍA ALEMANA

Plaza de Santa Ana 6 Ⓜ Sol or Antón Martín.
Mon & Wed–Sun 10.30am–12.30am, Fri & Sat
till 2am. Closed Aug. MAP P.54, POCKET MAP F13

Refurbished but still stylish old beer house, once frequented by Hemingway. Order a *caña* (draught beer) and go easy on the tapas, as the bill can mount up fast.

CERVECERÍA SANTA ANA

Plaza de Santa Ana 10 Ⓜ Sol or Antón
Martín. Daily 11am–1.30am, Fri & Sat till
2.30am. MAP P.54, POCKET MAP F13

Has tables outside, and offers quality beer, friendly service and a good selection of tapas. Always packed at night.

CÍRCULO DE BELLAS ARTES

C/Alcalá 42 Ⓜ Banco de España.
Daily 8am–2am, Fri & Sat till 3am. MAP P.54,
POCKET MAP G11

Great bar in this classy arts centre (€1 entry fee), complete with reclining nude sculpture, chandeliers and sofas and a pleasant lack of pretensions. Service can be slow though. From May to October there's a comfortable *terraza* outside.

DOS GARDENIAS

C/Santa María 13 Ⓜ Antón Martín. Mon–Sat
8pm–2.30am, Sun 5pm–2.30am. MAP P.54,
POCKET MAP G14

Intimate and relaxed little bar in the Huertas area where you can chill out in their comfy chairs, sip on a mojito, and escape from the hubbub of the city outside.

GLASS BAR

Carrera San Jerónimo 34 Ⓜ Sevilla. Daily
11am–3am. MAP P.54, POCKET MAP F12

Housed in the ultra-chic *Hotel Urban*, this glamorous cocktail bar has become a compulsory stop for the well-heeled in-crowd. Designer tapas such as sushi, wild salmon and oysters accompany drinks. In summer a terrace bar opens on the sixth floor.

NATURBIER

Plaza de Santa Ana 9 Ⓜ Sol or Antón Martín.
Daily 8pm–2.30am. MAP P.54, POCKET MAP F13

Try this place's own tasty beer with a variety of German sausages to accompany it. There's usually room to sit in the cellar if the top bar is too crowded, although service is often slow.

LA VENENCIA

C/Echegaray 7 Ⓜ Sevilla. Daily 7.30pm–1.30am.
Closed Aug. MAP P.54, POCKET MAP F12

Rather dilapidated, wood-panelled bar that's great for sherry sampling. The whole range is here, served from wooden barrels, and accompanied by delicious olives and *mojama* (dry salted tuna).

CÍRCULO DE BELLAS ARTES CAFÉ

VIVA MADRID

C/Manuel Fernández y González 7 Ⓜ Antón
Martín or Sevilla.Daily noon–2am, Fri & Sat
till 3am. MAP P.54, POCKET MAP F12

A fabulous tiled bar with
a popular terrace that is a
longtime stalwart of the
Madrid night scene. Remodelled in 2011 and now offering
a wide selection of food and
tapas, but still best for a drink.

Clubs

LA BOCA DEL LOBO

C/Echegaray 11 Ⓜ Antón Martín or Sevilla
Ⓦ www.labocadellobo.com. Tues–Sat
9.30pm–3am. MAP P.54, POCKET MAP F12

Dark, cavern-like club on this
buzzing little street close to
Santa Ana playing everything
from electronic and funk to
rock and salsa. Live gigs (in
the dungeon-like cellar) and
resident DJs.

STELLA

C/Arlabán 7 Ⓜ Sevilla Ⓦ www.web-mondo.
com. Thurs–Sat midnight–6am. Entrance
€12–15 including first drink. MAP P.54, POCKET
MAP F11

Unrecognizable from its days
as a Movida classic, *Stella* is
now a sleek modern club with
transparent dancefloor. It
remains a big favourite with
the city's serious party-goers,
especially for *El Fabuloso Club*
(Fri) and *Mondo* (Thurs & Sat)
sessions.

TORERO

C/Cruz 26 Ⓜ Sol. Tues–Sat 11pm–5.30am
(4.30am Wed). Entrance €10 including first
drink. MAP P.54, POCKET MAP E13

Popular two-floored club right
in the heart of the Santa Ana
area. The bouncers are pretty
strict, but once inside a fun
place to be. Music ranges from
salsa to disco.

STELLA

Live music

CAFÉ CENTRAL

Plaza del Ángel 10 Ⓜ Tirso de Molina
☎ 913 694 143 Ⓦ www.cafecentralmadrid
.com. Mon–Sat 1pm–1.30am, Fri & Sat till
2.30am. €11–12 for gigs, otherwise free.
MAP P.54, POCKET MAP E13

Small jazz club that gets the
odd big name, plus strong
local talent. The Art Deco
café (lunchtime menu €11.50;
€14.50 at weekends) is worth a
visit in its own right.

CAFÉ JAZZ POPULART

C/Huertas 22 Ⓜ Tirso de Molina ☎ 914 298
407 Ⓦ www.populart.es. Daily 6pm–2.30am.
Usually free. MAP P.54, POCKET MAP E13

Friendly and laidback venue,
with twice-nightly sets (11pm
& 12.30am) usually from jazz
and blues bands.

CARDAMOMO

C/Echegaray 15 Ⓜ Antón Martín or Sevilla
☎ 913 690 757 Ⓦ www.cardamomo.es.
Daily 8pm–4am. Shows at 9pm. MAP P.54,
POCKET MAP F12

This flamenco bar has evolved
into a respected fully blown
tablao. The show with a drink
is €39, while dinner will set you
back an extra €33. Check the
website for the schedule.

Paseo del Arte and Retiro

Madrid's three world-class art galleries are all located within a kilometre of each other along what is known as the Paseo del Arte. The Prado, the most renowned of the three, houses an unequalled display of Spanish art, an outstanding Flemish collection and some impressive Italian work. The Thyssen-Bornemisza, based on one of the world's greatest private art collections, provides a dazzling excursion through Western art from the fourteenth to the late twentieth centuries. Finally, the Centro de Arte Reina Sofía displays contemporary art, including Picasso's iconic masterpiece *Guernica*. The area around the Paseo del Prado has two beautiful green spaces: the Jardines Botánicos and the Parque del Retiro, as well as lesser-known sights including the fascinating Real Fábrica de Tapices (Royal Tapestry Workshop) and the Museo Naval. It isn't an area renowned for its bars, restaurants and nightlife, but there are plenty of decent places for a drink or lunch.

MUSEO DEL PRADO

Ⓜ Atocha or Banco de España Ⓦ www .museodelprado.es. Mon–Sat 10am–8pm, Sun & hols 10am–7pm. €14, free Mon–Sat 6–8pm, Sun & hols 5–7pm and for under-18s. MAP P.68–69, POCKET MAP G13

The Prado is Madrid's premier tourist attraction and one of the oldest and greatest collections of art in the world, largely amassed by the Spanish royal family over the last two hundred years.

Tickets are purchased at the Puerta de Goya opposite the *Hotel Ritz* on C/Felipe IV and the entrance is round the back

GARDEN OF EARTHLY DELIGHTS

at the Puerta de los Jerónimos, which leads into the new extension. To avoid the large ticket queues, buy them from the museum website, though you will still have to collect them at the box office at the Puerta de Goya (separate fast-moving queue).

The museum, which has been given a new lease of life following the addition of a €152 million Rafael Moneo-designed extension, is set out according to national schools. To follow the route proposed by the museum bear right upon entering and head into the central hallway, the Sala de las Musas; from here you are guided through the collections on the ground floor before being directed upstairs.

The coverage of Spanish paintings begins with some striking twelfth-century Romanesque frescoes. Beyond is a stunning anthology that includes just about every significant Spanish painter from the adopted Cretan-born artist El Greco (Domenikos Theotokopoulos), who worked in Toledo in the 1570s, to Francisco de Goya, the outstanding painter of eighteenth-century Bourbon Spain. Don't miss the breath-taking collection of work by Diego Velázquez, including his masterpiece, *Las Meninas*.

No visit is complete without taking in Goya's deeply evocative works, *Dos de Mayo* and *Tres de Mayo*, and his disturbing series of murals known as the *Pinturas Negras* (*Black Paintings*) with their mix of witches, fights to the death and child-eating gods.

The Italian paintings include the most complete collec-tion by painters from the Venice School in any single museum, among them Titian's

MUSEO DEL PRADO

magnificent equestrian portrait, *Emperor Carlos V at Mühlberg*. There are also major works by Raphael and epic master-pieces from Tintoretto, Veronese and Caravaggio.

The early Flemish works are even more impressive and contain one of Hieronymus Bosch's greatest triptychs, the hallucinogenic *Garden of Earthly Delights*. Look out, too, for the works of Pieter Bruegel the Elder, whose *Triumph of Death* must be one of the most frightening canvases ever painted, Rogier van der Weyden's magnificent *Descent from the Cross* and the exten-sive Rubens collection.

German and French painting is less well represented but still worth seeking out – especially the pieces by Dürer, Cranach and Poussin – while downstairs in the basement is a glittering display of the jewels that belonged to the Grand Dauphin Louis, son of Louis XIV and father of Felipe V, Spain's first Bourbon king.

The new wing houses temporary exhibition spaces, restoration workshops and a sculpture gallery as well as a restaurant, café and shops.

Paseo del Arte and Retiro

ACCOMMODATION

Chic & Basic Atocha	10
Hostal Gonzalo	6
Hotel Lope de Vega	7
Hotel Mora	9
Hotel Palace	4
Hotel Villa Real	3
Hotel Vincci Soma	1
NH Alcalá	2
NH Nacional	11
NH Paseo del Prado	5
Radisson Blu, Madrid Prado	8

SHOPPING

Cuesta Moyano	3
Objetos de Arte Toledano	1
Piel del Toro	2

CLUBS

Alegoría/Alquimia	1
Kapital	2

*Map labels:*

PLAZA DE LA VILLA DE PARIS · COLÓN · PLAZA DE COLÓN · Teatro Fernán Gómez · Jardines Descubrimiento · SERRANO · Las Salesas Reales · Palacio de Justicia · Museo de Cera · Biblioteca Nacional & Museo del Libro · Museo Arqueológico Nacional · C/JORGE JUAN · C/BÁRBARA DE BRAGANZA · PASEO DE RECOLETOS · CALLE VILLANUEVA · C/GIL DE SANTIVAÑES · CALLE CLAUDIO COELLO · C/CONDE DE XIQUENA · CALLE ALMIRANTE · CALLE PRIM · CALLE RECOLETOS · CALLE SERRANO · Palacio del Marqués de Salamanca · Palacio de Buenavista · C/MARQUÉS DEL DUERO · C/SALUSTIANO OLOZAGA · PLAZA DE LA INDEPENDENCIA · Puerta de Alcalá · AVENIDA · Palacio de Linares · PLAZA CIBELES · CALLE ALCALÁ · Fuente de la Cibeles · C/VALENZUELA · C/ALCALÁ · BANCO DE ESPAÑA · Palacio de Cibeles · Banco de España · Museo Postal · CALLE MONTALBÁN · Museo de Artes Decorativas · Círculo de Bellas Artes · CALLE LOS MADRAZO · Museo Naval · CALLE ALFONSO XII · C/JUAN DE MENA · PASEO · Teatro de la Zarzuela · Bolsa de Comercio · PLAZA DE LA LEALTAD · Monumento a los Caídos por España · C/ANTONIO MAURA · CARRERA SAN JERÓNIMO · Congreso de los Diputados · Museo Thyssen-Bornemisza · C/MÉNDEZ NÚÑEZ · Salón de Reinos · Ateneo Artístico, Científico y Literario · PLAZA DE LAS CORTES · Fuente de Neptuno · Hotel Ritz · C/MÉNDEZ NÚÑEZ · C/FELIPE IV · C/PRADO · Casa de Lope de Vega · PL CÁNOVAS DEL CASTILLO · CALLE FELIPE VI · Real Academia de la Lengua · Casón del Buen Retiro · CALLE CERVANTES · Jesús de Medinaceli · C/LOPE DE VEGA · San Jerónimo el Real · CALLE ACADEMIA · C/CASADO DEL ALISAL · ANTÓN MARTÍN · Convento Trinitarias Descalzas · C/ALBERTO BOSCH · PASEO · CALLE HUERTAS · Museo del Prado · CALLE RUIZ DE ALARCÓN · CALLE MORATÍN · PLAZA DE LA PLATERÍA DE MARTÍNEZ · CALLE ESPALTER · PLAZA DE MURILLO · Bosque de los Ausentes · C/GOBERNADOR · C/VERÓNICA · CaixaForum Madrid · Jardínes Botánicos · Pabellón Villanueva · CALLE ATOCHA · CUESTA CLAUDIO MOYANO · ATOCHA · Convento de Santa Isabel · Centro de Arte Reina Sofía · GLORIETA DEL EMPERADOR CARLOS V · Ministerio de Agricultura · PASEO LA INFANTA ISABEL · Observatorio Astronómico · Museo de Antropología/Etnología · RONDA ATOCHA · Antigua Estación de Atocha · AVENIDA LA CIUDAD DE BARCELONA · Monumento a las Víctimas del 11-M · ATOCHA RENFE · Estación de Atocha (AVE) · PASEO DE LAS DELICIAS

	metres	200
0		
0	yards	200

N

PASEO DEL ARTE AND RETIRO

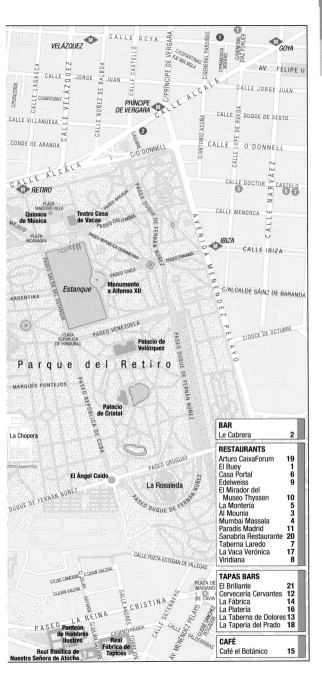

BAR

Le Cabrera	2

RESTAURANTS

Arturo CaixaForum	19
El Buey	1
Casa Portal	6
Edelweiss	9
El Mirador del Museo Thyssen	10
La Montería	5
Al Mounia	3
Mumbai Massala	4
Paradís Madrid	11
Sanabria Restaurante	20
Taberna Laredo	7
La Vaca Verónica	17
Viridiana	8

TAPAS BARS

El Brillante	21
Cervecería Cervantes	12
La Fábrica	14
La Platería	16
La Taberna de Dolores	13
La Tapería del Prado	18

CAFÉ

Café el Botánico	15

CENTRO DE ARTE REINA SOFÍA

Atocha ⓦ www.museoreinasofia.es. Mon & Wed–Sat 10am–9pm, Sun 10am–7pm. €8, free Mon, Wed–Sat 7–9pm, Sun after 3pm and for under-18s and over-65s. MAP P.68–69, POCKET MAP G8

An essential stop on the Madrid art circuit is the Centro de Arte Reina Sofía, an immense exhibition space providing a permanent home for the Spanish collection of modern and contemporary art, including the Miró and Picasso legacies.

If the queues at the main entrance are too long, try the alternative one in the extension on the Ronda de Atocha.

As well as its collection of twentieth-century art, the museum has a theatre, cinema, excellent bookshops, a print, music and photographic library, a restaurant, bar and café in the basement and a peaceful inner courtyard garden. An informative, but expensive, guidebook examining some of the key works is available from the shops, priced €22. At the entrance, there are audio-guides in English (€4), which provide informative commentaries for the first-time visitor.

The **permanent collection** begins on the second floor with a section examining the origins of modern Spanish art, largely through the two artistic nuclei that developed in Catalunya and the Basque Country at the end of the nineteenth century.

Midway round the collection is the Reina Sofía's main draw – Picasso's *Guernica* (see box opposite), an emblematic piece that has always evoked strong reactions. Strong sections on Cubism in the first of which Picasso is again well represented – and the Paris School follow. Dalí and Miró make heavyweight contributions too in the Surrealism section, and there is an impressive collection of Spanish sculpture.

The collection continues on the fourth floor, although here it's no match for the attractions of the previous exhibits. This section covers Spain's postwar years up to 1968 and includes Spanish and international examples of abstract and avant-garde movements such as Pop Art, Constructivism and Minimalism, one of the highlights being Francis Bacon's *Figura Tumbada* (*Reclining Figure*). Worth hunting out is the section on photography during the years of Franco's dictatorship, and the work by British artists Henry Moore and Graham Sutherland.

There are also some striking pieces by the Basque abstract sculptor Chillida and Catalan Surrealist painter Antoni Tàpies. The fourth-floor galleries finish on a high with more offerings from Picasso and Miró, including the former's *El pintor y la modelo* (The Painter and the Model, 1963) series, painted when he was over 80 years old.

Jean Nouvel's 79 million-euro state-of-the-art extension, known as the **Area Nouvel**, is built around an open courtyard topped by a striking delta-shaped, metallic, crimson-

I f you plan to visit all three art museums on the Paseo del Prado during your stay, it's well worth buying the **Paseo del Arte ticket** (€21.60), which is valid for a year and allows one visit to each museum at a substantial saving although it does not include the temporary exhibitions. It's available at any of the three museums.

coloured roof. It now houses the third part of the collection covering the period 1962–1982, with a focus on experimental, revolutionary and feminist art. It includes some striking photographic art on the Battle of Algiers and Cuban Revolution. The new wing is also home to temporary exhibition spaces, an auditorium, library, bookshop and café-restaurant.

Guernica

Superbly displayed and no longer protected by the bullet-proof glass and steel girders that once imprisoned it, Picasso's *Guernica* is a monumental icon of twentieth-century Spanish art and politics which, despite its familiarity, still has the ability to shock. Picasso painted it in response to the bombing of the Basque town of Gernika in April 1937 by the German Luftwaffe, acting in concert with Franco, during the Spanish Civil War. In the preliminary studies, displayed around the room, you can see how he developed its symbols – the dying horse, the woman mourning, the bull and so on – and then return to the painting to marvel at how he made it all work. Picasso determined that the work be "loaned" to the Museum of Modern Art in New York while Franco remained in power, meaning that the artist never lived to see it displayed in his home country – it only returned to Spain in 1981, eight years after Picasso's death and six after the demise of Franco.

MUSEO THYSSEN-BORNEMISZA

Ⓜ Banco de España ⓦ www.museothyssen
.org. Mon noon–4pm, Tues–Sun 10am–7pm.
€9 for permanent collection, €8–10 for
temporary exhibitions, combined ticket
€12–15, permanent collection free Mon. MAP
P.68–69, POCKET MAP H12

MUSEO THYSSEN-BORNEMISZA

This fabulous private collection, assembled by Baron Heinrich Thyssen-Bornemisza, his son Hans Heinrich and his former beauty-queen wife Carmen was first displayed here in 1993 and contains pieces by almost every major Western artist since the fourteenth century.

An extension, built on the site of an adjoining mansion and cleverly integrated into the original format of the museum, houses temporary exhibitions and Carmen's collection, which is particularly strong on nineteenth-century landscape, North American, Impressionist and Post-Impressionist work.

To follow the collection chronologically, begin on the second floor with pre-Renaissance work from the fourteenth century. This is followed by a wonderful array of Renaissance portraits by, amongst others, Ghirlandaio, Raphael and Holbein, including the latter's commanding *Henry VIII*. Beyond are some equally impressive pieces by Titian, Tintoretto, El Greco, Caravaggio and Canaletto, while a superb collection of landscapes and some soothing Impressionist works by Pissarro, Monet, Renoir, Degas and Sisley are housed in the new galleries.

The first floor continues with an outstanding selection of work by Gauguin and the Post-Impressionists. There's excellent coverage, too, of the vivid Expressionist work of Kandinsky, Nolde and Kirchner.

Beyond, the displays include a comprehensive round of seventeenth-century Dutch painting of various genres and some splendid nineteenth-century American landscapes. There are strong contributions from Van Gogh – most notably one of his last and most gorgeous works, *Les Vessenots* – and more from the Expressionists, including the apocalyptic *Metropolis* by George Grosz.

The ground floor covers the period from the beginning of the twentieth century with some outstanding Cubist work from Picasso, Braque and Mondrian to be found within the "experimental avant-garde" section. There are also some marvellous pieces by Miró, Pollock and Chagall. Surrealism is, not surprisingly, represented by Dalí, while the final galleries include some eye-catching work by Bacon, Lichtenstein and Freud.

PARQUE DEL RETIRO

Ⓜ Retiro, Ibiza, Atocha Renfe, Atocha or Banco de España. MAP P.68–69, POCKET MAP K4–K7

The origins of the wonderful Parque del Retiro (Retiro Park) go back to the early seventeenth century when Felipe IV produced a plan for a new palace and French-style gardens, the Buen Retiro. Of the buildings, only the ballroom

(Casón del Buen Retiro) and the Hall of Realms (the Salón de Reinos) remain.

The park's 330-acre expanse offers the chance to jog, roller-blade, cycle, picnic, row on the lake, have your fortune told, and – above all – **promenade**. The busiest day is Sunday, when half of Madrid turns out for the *paseo*.

Promenading aside, there's almost always something going on in the park, including concerts in the Quiosco de Música, performances by groups of South American pan-piping musicians by the lake and, on summer weekends, puppet shows by the Puerta de Alcalá entrance.

Travelling art exhibitions are frequently housed in the graceful **Palacio de Velázquez** (daily: April–Sept 10am–10pm; Oct–March 10am–6pm; free) and the splendid **Palacio de Cristal** (same hours during exhibitions, but closed when raining; free), while the **Teatro Casa de Vacas** (Ⓦwww.casade-vacas.es) hosts shows, concerts and plays. Look out, too, for

the magnificently ostenta-tious statue to Alfonso XII by the lake and the Ángel Caído, supposedly the world's only public statue to Lucifer, in the south of the park. The Bosque de los Ausentes, 192 olive trees and cypresses planted by the Paseo de la Chopera in memory of the victims who died in the train bombings at the nearby Atocha station on March 11, 2004, is close by.

PUERTA DE ALCALÁ

Ⓜ Retiro or Banco de España. MAP P.68–69, POCKET MAP J4

The Puerta de Alcalá is one of Madrid's most emblematic landmarks. Built in neoclassical style in 1769 by Francesco Sabatini to commemorate Carlos III's first twenty years on the throne, it was the biggest city gate in Europe at the time. Once on the site of the city's easternmost boundary, it's now marooned on a small island on the traffic-choked Plaza de la Independencia.

JARDÍNES BOTÁNICOS

Plaza de Murillo 2 Ⓜ Atocha Ⓦwww.rjb.csic.es. Daily 10am–dusk. €3, under-10s free. MAP P.68–69, POCKET MAP H7

The delightful botanical gardens were opened in 1781 by Carlos III. The king's aim was to collect and grow species from all over his Spanish Empire, develop a research centre, and supply medicinal herbs and plants to Madrid's hospitals. Abandoned for much of the last century, they were restored in the 1980s and are now home to some 30,000 species from around the globe. Don't miss the hothouse with its amazing cacti or the bonsai collection of former prime minister Felipe González. Temporary exhibi-tions take place in the Pabellón Villanueva within the grounds.

PARQUE DEL RETIRO

PASEO DEL ARTE AND RETIRO

CAIXAFORUM MADRID

Paseo del Prado 36 Ⓜ Atocha. Daily 10am–8pm. Free. MAP P.68–69, POCKET MAP H7

An innovative exhibition space, opened in 2008 by the Catalan savings bank, which complements the existing attractions on the Paseo del Arte. The centre, which hosts a variety of high-quality art shows, is flanked by an eye-catching **vertical garden** designed by French botanist Patrick Blanc in which some 15,000 plants form an organic carpet extending across the wall. There is a decent art bookshop inside and a top-floor café/ restaurant (see p.77).

MUSEO DE ARTES DECORATIVAS

C/Montalbán 12 Ⓜ Banco de España Ⓦ mnartesdecorativas.mcu.es. Tues–Sat 9.30am–3pm, Sun 10am–3pm, plus Thurs 5–8pm Sept–June. €3, free on Sun and Thurs eve. MAP P.68–69, POCKET MAP J5

The national collection of decorative arts is housed in an elegant nineteenth-century mansion. The highlight is its collection of *azulejos* (tiles) and other ceramics with a magnificent eighteenth-century tiled Valencian kitchen on the top floor. The rest of the exhibits include an interesting but unspectacular collection of furniture, a series of reconstructed rooms and *objets d'art* from all over Spain.

MUSEO NAVAL

Paseo del Prado 5 Ⓜ Banco de España Ⓦ armada.mde.es. Tues–Sun 10am–7pm; closed public hols. Free (bring ID). MAP P.68–69, POCKET MAP J11

As you might expect, the Naval Museum is strong on models, charts and navigational aids relating to Spanish voyages of discovery. Exhibits include the first map to show the New World, drawn in 1500 by Juan de la Cosa, cannons from the Spanish Armada and part of Cortés' standard used during the conquest of Mexico. The room dedicated to the *Nao San Diego*, sunk during a conflict with the Dutch off the Philippines in 1600, contains fascinating items recovered during the salvage operation in the early 1990s.

SAN JERÓNIMO EL REAL

C/Ruiz de Alarcón 19 Ⓜ Atocha or Banco de España. Mon–Sat 10am–1pm & 5–8.30pm, Sun & hols 9.30am–2.30pm & 5.30–8.30pm. MAP P.68–69, POCKET MAP H6

Madrid's high-society church was built on the site of a monastery founded in the early sixteenth century by the

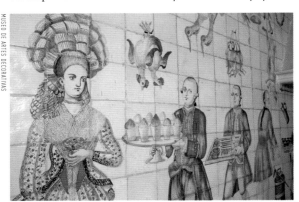
MUSEO DE ARTES DECORATIVAS

early sixteenth century by the Catholic monarchs, Fernando and Isabel. It later became the venue for the swearing-in of the heirs to the throne and setting for many royal marriages and coronations (including the current king, Juan Carlos in 1975). Despite remodelling and the addition of two Gothic towers, the old form of the church is still visible; but the seventeenth-century cloisters have fallen victim to the Prado extension.

PLAZA DE LA LEALTAD (MONUMENTO A LOS CAÍDOS POR ESPAÑA)

Ⓜ Banco de España. MAP P.68–69, POCKET MAP H6
This aristocratic plaza contains the **Monument to Spain's Fallen**. Originally a memorial to the Madrileños who died in the 1808 anti-French rebellion (the urn at the base contains their ashes), it was later changed to commemorate all those who have died fighting for Spain, and an eternal flame now burns here. On one side of the plaza stands the opulent *Ritz Hotel*, work of Charles Mewès, architect of the *Ritz* hotels in Paris and London, while opposite is the Madrid stock exchange.

ESTACIÓN DE ATOCHA

Ⓜ Atocha or Atocha Renfe. MAP P.68–69, POCKET MAP J9
The grand Estación de Atocha is now sadly infamous as the scene of the horrific train bombings that killed 191 people and injured close to 2000 in March 2004. A glass memorial to the victims stands just outside one of the entrances on Paseo de la Infanta Isabel. The tower channels light into an underground chamber (access via the station) lined with an inner membrane on which are

MONUMENTO A LOS CAÍDOS POR ESPAÑA

written messages of condolence. The old station alongside was revamped in 1992 and is a glorious 1880s glasshouse, resembling a tropical garden. It's a wonderful sight from the walkways above, as a constant spray of water rains down on the jungle of vegetation. At the platforms beyond sit the gleaming AVE trains.

MUSEO NACIONAL DE ANTROPOLOGÍA/ETNOLOGÍA

C/Alfonso XII 68 Ⓜ Atocha or Atocha Renfe Ⓦ mnantropologia.mcu.es.Tues–Sat 9.30am–8pm, Sun 10am–3pm. €3, free Sat after 2pm & Sun. MAP P.68–69, POCKET MAP J8
The National Anthropology and Ethnography Museum was founded by the eccentric Dr Pedro González Velasco to house his private collection. The displays give an overview of different cultures, particu-larly those linked to Spanish history. The most interesting exhibits include a macabre collection of deformed skulls, a Guanche mummy (the original inhabitants of the Canary Islands), some shrivelled embryos and the skeleton of a 2.35m tall circus giant, which Velasco had agreed to buy from the owner after his death – payment in advance of course.

REAL FÁBRICA DE TAPICES

REAL FÁBRICA DE TAPICES

C/Fuentarrabía 2 Ⓜ Atocha Renfe or
Menéndez Pelayo Ⓦ www.realfabricade
tapices.com. Mon–Fri 10am–2pm; closed
Aug. €4. Tours every half-hour. MAP P.68–69,
POCKET MAP K9

The Royal Tapestry Workshop
makes for a fascinating visit.
Founded in 1721 and moved
to its present site in the
nineteenth century, the factory
uses processes and machines
unchanged for hundreds of
years. The handful of workers
that remain can be seen coolly
looping handfuls of bobbins
around myriad strings and
sewing up worn-out master-
pieces with exact matching
silk. With progress painfully
slow – one worker produces a
square metre of tapestry every
three and a half months – the
astronomical prices soon seem
easily understandable.

Shops

CUESTA MOYANO

Cuesta de Claudio Moyano Ⓜ Atocha.
MAP P.68–69, POCKET MAP H8

A row of little wooden kiosks
on a hill close to the Retiro
selling just about every book
you could think of, from
second-hand copies of Captain
Marvel to Cervantes. Other
items include old prints of
Madrid and relics from the
Franco era.

OBJETOS DE ARTE TOLEDANO

Paseo del Prado 10 Ⓜ Atocha or Banco de
España. Mon–Sat 10am–8pm. MAP P.68–69,
POCKET MAP H13

Souvenir shop stocking "typical
Spanish"-style goods including
fans, Lladró porcelain, T-shirts
and tacky flamenco accessories.

PIEL DEL TORO

Paseo del Prado 42 Ⓜ Atocha or Banco de
España. Mon–Fri 10am–8.30pm, Sat & Sun
11am–8pm. MAP P.68–69, POCKET MAP H7

A colourful range of T-shirts,
sweatshirts and baseball
caps, all emblazoned with the
emblem of a bull. Despite the
clichéd image they make good,
lightweight presents.

Café

CAFÉ EL BOTÁNICO

C/Ruiz de Alarcón 27 Ⓜ Atocha or Banco
de España. Daily 9am–midnight. MAP P.68–69,
POCKET MAP H7

An ideal place for a coffee or
drink after a Prado visit; it sits
in a quiet street next to the
botanical gardens and serves
good beer and a small selection
of tapas. Service can be slow.

Restaurants

ARTURO CAIXAFORUM

Paseo del Prado 36 Ⓜ Banco de España
☎ 913 896 795. Daily 10am–8pm. MAP P.68–69,
POCKET MAP H7

Located in a stylish arts centre, this café/restaurant combines designer decor with well-presented Mediterranean-style food. Prices are reasonable if you opt for the €12 lunchtime menu which includes a choice of three dishes for each course.

EL BUEY

C/General Diaz Porlier 9 Ⓜ Goya
☎ 914 314 492. Mon–Sat 1–4pm &
9pm–midnight, Sun 1–4pm. MAP P.68–69,
POCKET MAP K3

Top-quality meat and excellent side dishes in this friendly little restaurant near the Retiro. Prices – €30 a head – are decent considering the quality.

CASA PORTAL

C/Dr Castelo 26 Ⓜ Ibiza ☎ 915 742 026.
Tues 1.30–4pm, Wed–Sat 1.30–4pm &
8.30–11.30pm. Closed hols & Aug. MAP P.68–69,
POCKET MAP K4

Despite a change of ownership, *Casa Portal* retains its reputation for superlative Asturian cooking – go for the *fabada* (beans, *chorizo* and black pudding stew) or *besugo* (bream), washed down with some cider. The shellfish is excellent too. Around €35–40 per person.

EDELWEISS

C/Jovellanos 7 Ⓜ Banco de España
☎ 915 323 383. 1–4pm & 8pm–midnight,
closed Sun eve. MAP P.68–69, POCKET MAP G11

Renowned German restaurant with an array of central European specialities and large portions. Expect to pay around €35 a head, although there's a €20 lunchtime menu including *Bratwurst*.

EL MIRADOR DEL MUSEO THYSSEN

Paseo del Prado 8 Ⓜ Banco de España ☎ 914 293 984. Tues–Sat 8.30pm–2.30am July & Aug only. MAP P.68–69, POCKET MAP H12

Summer-only terrace restaurant on the top floor of the art museum with some great views over the city. Specializes in Mediterranean cuisine; dishes include smoked salmon with pear paté. Reservations essential; €40–50 a head.

LA MONTERÍA

C/Lope de Rueda 35 Ⓜ Ibiza ☎ 915 741 812.
Mon–Sat 2–4pm & 8.30pm–11pm. MAP P.68–69,
POCKET MAP K4

This inconspicuous little restaurant on the Retiro's eastern edge was recently revamped, and serves some of the tastiest food in the area. The speciality *salmorejo* is excellent, as are the battered prawns, while mains include partridge and monkfish options. At least €35 a head.

AL MOUNIA

C/Recoletos 5 Ⓜ Banco de España
☎ 914 350 828. Tues–Sat 1.30–3.30pm &
9pm–midnight. Closed Aug. MAP P.68–69, POCKET
MAP H4

Moroccan cooking at its best in the most established Arabic restaurant in town. The couscous, lamb and desserts are a must. Mains cost over €20; lunchtime menus start at €37.

MUMBAI MASSALA

C/Recoletos 14 Ⓜ Banco de España or Retiro ☎ 914 357 194. Daily 1.30–4pm & 9–11.30pm. MAP P.68–69, POCKET MAP J4

The decor is palatial in this upmarket Indian restaurant, serving a wide range of very good, but expensive, curries – all the usual favourites are available. Evening prices are in the region of €40 a head, but a better alternative is the lunchtime menu for just €14.75.

VIRIDIANA

PARADÍS MADRID

C/Marqués de Cubas 14 Ⓜ Banco de
España ☎ 914 297 303. Mon–Fri 1–4pm &
8.30pm–midnight, Sat eve only. MAP P.68–69,
POCKET MAP H12

Upmarket Catalan restaurant
often frequented by politicians
from the nearby parliament.
High-quality Mediterranean
food with superb starters,
fish and rice dishes. Expect to
pay around €50.

SANABRIA RESTAURANTE

C/Doctor Mata 3 Ⓜ Atocha ☎ 914 673 390.
Daily 8am–midnight. MAP P.68–69, POCKET MAP H8

Great-value restaurant just
around the corner from the
Reina Sofía. Six choices for
each course of the *menú del
día*, generous helpings and a
very filling *fabada* (bean stew).

TABERNA LAREDO

C/Dr Castelo 30 Ⓜ Ibiza ☎ 915 733 061.
Mon–Sat 11am–5pm & 8pm–midnight. Closed
Aug. MAP P.68–69, POCKET MAP K4

Delicious salads, risottos and
fish dishes served up with style
at this acclaimed bar/restaurant
close to the Retiro. The €42
sampler menu is a very good
option. Reservations essential.

LA VACA VERÓNICA

C/Moratín 38 Ⓜ Antón Martín
☎ 914 297 827. Mon–Sat 1–4.30pm &
8.30pm–12.30am, Sun 1–4.30pm. MAP P.68–69,
POCKET MAP H14

A wide range of dishes at this
slightly bohemian little restaurant. Try the *filet Verónica* and
the *carabinero con pasta* (pasta
with red prawns). The *menú* is
€15 (evening/weekend €20).

VIRIDIANA

C/Juan de Mena 14 Ⓜ Banco de España
☎ 915 234 478 or 915 311 039. Mon–Sat
1.45–4pm & 8.30pm–midnight. Closed Easter
& Aug. MAP P.68–69, POCKET MAP J6

A bizarre temple of Madrid
nueva cocina (new cuisine),
decorated with photos from
Luis Buñuel's film of the same
name and offering mouthwa-
tering creations, plus a superb
selection of wines. The bill for
a three-course meal is likely to
come close to €100 a head but
it's an unforgettable experience.

Tapas bars

EL BRILLANTE

Glorieta del Emperador Carlos V 8
Ⓜ Atocha. Daily 6.30am–12.30am. MAP P.68–69,
POCKET MAP H8

Down-to-earth bar with long
opening hours and a range
of tapas and *bocadillos* (filled
baguette). *Calamares* is the
house special. Good for a snack
in between museum visits.

CERVECERÍA CERVANTES

Plaza de Jesús 7 Ⓜ Antón Martín or
Banco de España. Mon–Sat 12.30–5pm &
7.30–11.45pm, Sun noon–4pm. MAP P.68–69,
POCKET MAP H13

Great beer and excellent fresh
seafood tapas in this busy little
bar just behind the *Palace
Hotel*. The *gambas* (prawns) go
down a treat with a cool glass
of the beer, while the *tosta de*

gambas (a sort of prawn toast) is a must.

LA FÁBRICA

Plaza de Jesús 2 Ⓜ Antón Martín or Banco de España. Mon–Thurs & Sun 11am–1am, Fri & Sat 11am–2am. MAP P.68–69, POCKET MAP H13

Bustling, friendly bar serving a delicious range of canapés, chilled beer and good vermouth.

LA PLATERÍA

C/Moratín 49 Ⓜ Antón Martín or Atocha. Mon–Fri 7.30am–1am, Sat & Sun 9.30am–1am. MAP P.68–69, POCKET MAP H14

This bar has a popular summer *terraza* geared to a tourist clientele and a good selection of reasonably priced tapas available all day. Service can be a little brusque though.

LA TABERNA DE DOLORES

Plaza de Jesús 4 Ⓜ Antón Martín or Banco de España. Daily 11am–midnight. MAP P.68–69, POCKET MAP H13

A standing-room-only tiled bar, decorated with beer bottles from around the world. The beer is great and the splendid food specialities include roquefort and anchovy and smoked-salmon canapés.

LA TAPERÍA DEL PRADO

Plaza Platerías de Martínez 1 Ⓜ Antón Martín or Banco de España ☎ 914 294 094. Mon–Thurs 8am–1am, Fri–Sun 10am–2am. MAP P.68–69, POCKET MAP J14

Modern bar serving up a range of tapas and *raciones*, plus a decent set lunch at around €10. Portions are on the small side.

Bars

LE CABRERA

C/Bárbara de Braganza 2 Ⓜ Colón. Daily 1.30–4pm & 8.30pm–midnight, Fri & Sat until 2.30am. MAP P.68–69, POCKET MAP H3

A chic bar serving drinks and creative tapas in the gastro bar on the ground floor and expertly mixed cocktails in the cosier basement area. There's another branch in the Casa de América at Paseo de Recoletos 2.

Clubs

ALEGORÍA/ALQUIMIA

C/Villanueva 2 (entrance on C/Cid) Ⓜ Colón ☎ 915 772 785 ⊕ www.alegoria-madrid.es. Thurs & Fri 9pm–5am, Sat 9pm–6am, Sun & Mon 9pm–2.30am. Entrance €9, free Thurs & Sun. MAP P.68–69, POCKET MAP J3

Modelled on an English gentleman's club, this restaurant, bar and disco comes complete with leather sofas, a wood-panelled library and models of old sailing ships hanging from the ceiling.

KAPITAL

C/Atocha 125 Ⓜ Atocha ⊕ www.grupo-kapital.com. Wed–Sat midnight–6am. From €12. MAP P.68–69, POCKET MAP H8

A seven-floor club catering for practically every taste, with three dancefloors, lasers, go-go dancers, a cinema and a *terraza*. The musical menu features disco, house, merengue, salsa, *sevillanas* and even the occasional session of karaoke.

ALEGORÍA

Gran Vía, Chueca and Malasaña

The Gran Vía, one of Madrid's main thoroughfares, effectively divides the old city to the south from the newer parts in the north. Heaving with traffic, shoppers and sightseers, it's the commercial heart of the city, and a monument in its own right, with its turn-of-the-twentieth-century, palace-like banks and offices. North of here, and bursting with bars, restaurants and nightlife, are two of the city's most vibrant barrios: Chueca, focal point of Madrid's gay scene, and Malasaña, former centre of the Movida Madrileña, the happening scene of the late 1970s and early 1980s, and still a somewhat alternative area, focusing on lively Plaza Dos de Mayo. As well as the bustling atmosphere, a couple of museums and a number of beautiful churches in the area provide even more reasons for a visit.

GRAN VÍA

Ⓜ Gran Vía. MAP P.82–83, POCKET MAP D10–G10

The Gran Vía (Great Way), built in three stages at the start of the twentieth century, became a symbol of Spain's arrival in the modern world. Financed on the back of an economic boom, experienced as a result of the country's neutrality in World War I, the Gran Vía is a showcase for a whole gamut of architectural styles, from Modernist to Neo-Rococo.

The finest section is the earliest, constructed between 1910 and 1924 and stretching from C/Alcalá to the Telefónica skyscraper. Particularly noteworthy are the Edificio Metrópolis (1905–11), complete with cylindrical facade, white

GRAN VÍA

stone sculptures, zinc-tiled roof and gold garlands, and the nearby Grassy building (1916–17). The vast 81m-high slab of the Telefónica building was Spain's first skyscraper. During the Civil War it was used as a reference point by Franco's forces to bomb the area. The stretch down to Plaza de Callao is dominated by shops, cafés and cinemas, while the plaza itself is now the gateway to the shoppers' haven of C/Preciados. On the corner is the classic Art Deco Capitol building (1930–33), its curved facade embellished with lurid neon signs. Cast your eyes skywards on the final stretch downhill towards Plaza de España to catch sight of an assortment of statues and decorations that top many of the buildings.

PLAZA DE CHUECA

PLAZA DE CHUECA

Ⓜ Chueca. MAP P.82–83, POCKET MAP G3

The smaller streets north of Gran Vía are home to all manner of vice-related activities and are notorious for petty crime. However, in Plaza de Chueca there's a strong neighbourhood feel and a lively gay scene at night. The area has been rejuvenated in recent years and now holds some enticing streets lined with offbeat restaurants, small private art galleries and unusual corner shops. Calle Almirante has some of the city's most fashionable clothes shops and Calle Augusto Figueroa is the place to go for shoes.

LAS SALESAS REALES

Plaza de las Salesas Ⓜ Colon. Mon–Fri 9am–1pm & 5–8pm, Sat & Sun 10am–2pm & 6–9pm. MAP P.82–83, POCKET MAP H3

The Santa Bárbara church was originally part of the convent complex of las Salesas Reales, founded in 1747. The church is set behind a fine forecourt,

while inside, there's a grotto-like chapel, delightful frescoes and stained-glass windows, and some striking green marble altar decoration. The tombs of Fernando VI, his wife Bárbara de Bragança and military hero General O'Donnell lie within.

SOCIEDAD DE AUTORES

C/Fernando VI 4 Ⓜ Alonso Martinez. MAP P.82–83, POCKET MAP G3

Home to the Society of Authors, this is the most significant Modernista building in Madrid. Designed in 1902 by the Catalan architect José Grasés Riera, its facade features a dripping decoration of flowers, faces and balconies.

PLAZA DEL DOS DE MAYO

Ⓜ Tribunal or Bilbao. MAP P.82–83, POCKET MAP E2

Plaza del Dos de Mayo is the centre of a lively bar scene, with people spilling onto the streets that converge on the square. The plaza commemorates the rebellion against occupying French troops in 1808, while the neighbourhood gets its name from a young seamstress, Manuela Malasaña, who became one of the rebellion's heroines.

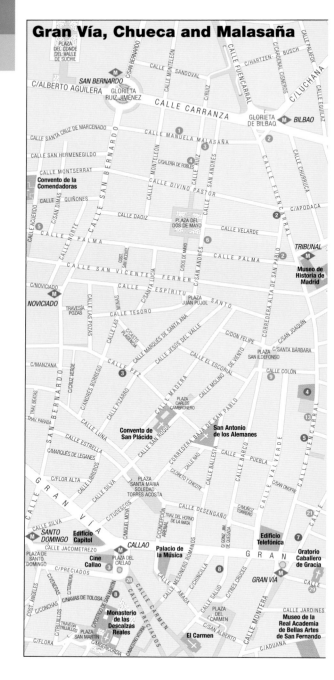

Gran Vía, Chueca and Malasaña

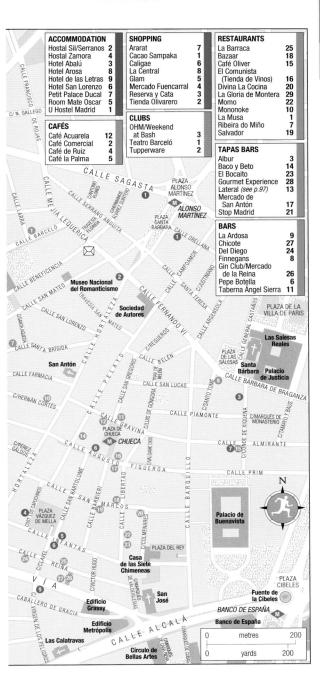

ACCOMMODATION

Hostal Sil/Serranos	2
Hostal Zamora	4
Hotel Abalú	3
Hotel Arosa	8
Hotel de las Letras	9
Hotel San Lorenzo	6
Petit Palace Ducal	7
Room Mate Oscar	5
U Hostel Madrid	1

CAFÉS

Café Acuarela	12
Café Comercial	2
Café de Ruiz	4
Café la Palma	5

SHOPPING

Ararat	7
Cacao Sampaka	1
Caligae	6
La Central	8
Glam	5
Mercado Fuencarral	4
Reserva y Cata	3
Tienda Olivarero	2

CLUBS

OHM/Weekend at Bash	3
Teatro Barceló	1
Tupperware	2

RESTAURANTS

La Barraca	25
Bazaar	18
Café Oliver	15
El Comunista (Tienda de Vinos)	16
Divina La Cocina	20
La Gloria de Montera	29
Momo	22
Mononoke	10
La Musa	1
Ribeira do Miño	7
Salvador	19

TAPAS BARS

Albur	3
Baco y Beto	14
El Bocaito	23
Gourmet Experience	28
Lateral (see p.97)	13
Mercado de San Antón	17
Stop Madrid	21

BARS

La Ardosa	9
Chicote	27
Del Diego	24
Finnegans	8
Gin Club/Mercado de la Reina	26
Pepe Botella	6
Taberna Ángel Sierra	11

83

MUSEO NACIONAL DEL ROMANTICISMO

C/San Mateo 13 🚇 Tribunal
🌐 museoromanticismo.mcu.es. May–Oct Tues–Sat 9.30am–8.30pm (closes 6.30pm Nov–April), Sun 10am–3pm. €3, free on Sat after 2pm, Sun. MAP P.82–83, POCKET MAP F2

The freshly renovated Museo del Romanticismo, aims to show the lifestyle and outlook of the late-Romantic era through the re-creation of a typical bourgeois residence in the turbulent reign of Isabel II (1833–1868), and this it does brilliantly. Overflowing with a marvellously eclectic and often kitsch hoard of memorabilia, the mansion is decorated with some stunning period furniture and ceiling frescoes, together with more bizarre exhibits such as the pistol which the satirist Mariano José de Larra used to shoot himself in 1837 after being spurned by his lover.

MUSEO DE HISTORIA DE MADRID

C/Fuencarral 78 🚇 Tribunal 🌐 www.munimadrid .es/museomunicipal. Tues–Sun 9.30am–8pm. Free. MAP P.82–83, POCKET MAP F2

Just around the corner from the Museo del Romanticismo, the Museo de Historia de Madrid is in the final throes of yet another lengthy restoration programme. The former city almshouse was remodelled in the early eighteenth century by Pedro de Ribera and features one of his trademark elaborately decorated Baroque doorways superimposed on a striking red brick facade. Inside, the museum contains a chronological collection of paintings, photos, models, sculptures and porcelain, all relating to the history and urban development of Madrid since 1561 (the date it was designated imperial capital by Felipe II). The centre-piece is a fascinating 3-D model of the city made in 1830 by military engineer León Gil de Palacio.

SAN ANTONIO DE LOS ALEMANES

Corredera de San Pablo 16 🚇 Chueca or Callao. Daily 11am–1pm & 6–8pm. Closed Aug. €2. MAP P.82–83, POCKET MAP E3

Opening hours are limited, coinciding with Mass, but this little church is one of the city's hidden treasures. Designed in 1624 by the Jesuit archi-tect Pedro Sánchez and Juan Gómez de Mora. The elliptical interior is lined with dizzying floor-to-ceiling pastel-coloured frescoes by Neapolitan artist Luca Giordano which depict scenes from the life of St Anthony.

SAN ANTONIO DE LOS ALEMANES

Shops

ARARAT

C/Almirante 10 Ⓜ Chueca. Mon–Sat
11am–2pm & 5–8.30pm. MAP P.82–83,
POCKET MAP G3

Spanish and foreign designers
for women at reasonable prices.
You can find formal and party
wear as well as younger styles.

CACAO SAMPAKA

C/Orellana 4 Ⓜ Alonso Martinez. Daily
10am–9.30pm; closed Aug 8–21. MAP P.82–83,
POCKET MAP G2

There's every conceivable
colour, shape and flavour
of chocolate here. The only
surprise is that their restaurant has some non-chocolate
options on the menu.

CALIGAE

C/Augusto Figueroa 27 Ⓜ Chueca.
Mon–Fri 10am–2pm & 5–8pm, Sat
10.30am–2pm & 5–8pm. MAP P.82–83,
POCKET MAP G3

One of a string of shoe shops
on this busy Chueca street
selling discounted designer
footwear. If you're on the
lookout for some sandals,
fashion trainers, party shoes
or boots, then this is the place
to come.

LA CENTRAL

C/Postigo de San Martín 8 Ⓜ Callao.
Mon–Fri 9.30am–10pm, Sat 10am–10pm, Sun
10am–9.30pm. MAP P.82–83, POCKET MAP C10

Stunning new bookshop
over four floors of a beautifully decorated building just
off Plaza Callao. As well as
thumbing your way through
copies of its comprehen-
sive selection of Spanish,
Latin American and English
classics you can admire the
frescoed ceilings, check out the
basement cocktail bar or have a
drink in the café.

GLAM

GLAM

C/Fuencarral 35 Ⓜ Gran Vía. Mon–Fri
11am–9pm, Sat 11am–9.30pm, Sun
4.30–9pm. MAP P.82–83, POCKET MAP F3

Club/street-style clothes that
wouldn't look out of place in an
Almodóvar film. There's a shoe
shop with wacky trainers and
trendy footwear next door.

MERCADO FUENCARRAL

C/Fuencarral 45 Ⓜ Gran Vía. Mon–Sat
10am–10pm. MAP P.82–83, POCKET MAP F3

Shopping mall filled with
clubwear shops, record stores,
jewellers, a café and even a
tattoo parlour.

RESERVA Y CATA

C/Conde de Xiquena 13 Ⓜ Chueca. Mon
5–9pm, Tues–Fri 11am–3pm & 5–9pm, Sat
11am–3pm. MAP P.82–83, POCKET MAP G3

Staff at this friendly specialist
shop will help you select from
some of the best new wines in
the Iberian peninsula. They
offer wine tasting sessions too.

TIENDA OLIVARERO

C/Mejia Lequerica 1 Ⓜ Alonso Martinez.
Mon–Fri 10am–2pm & 5–8pm, Sat
10am–2pm. MAP P.82–83, POCKET MAP G2

This olive-growers' co-operative
outlet has useful information
sheets to help you buy the best
olive oils from around Spain.

Cafés

CAFÉ ACUARELA

C/Gravina 10 Ⓜ Chueca. Daily 2pm–2am. MAP
P.82–83, POCKET MAP G3

Comfy café, with over-the-
top Baroque decor and great
cocktails. Popular with a mostly
gay/lesbian crowd.

CAFÉ COMERCIAL

Glorieta de Bilbao 7 Ⓜ Bilbao. Daily
8am–1am, Fri & Sat till 2am. MAP P.82–83,
POCKET MAP F1

A Madrileño institution and
one of the city's most popular
meeting points, this is a lovely
traditional café full of mirrors,
large tables and a cross-section
of Madrid society. Free wi-fi
too.

CAFÉ DE RUIZ

C/Ruiz 11 Ⓜ Bilbao. Daily 11am–2am.
MAP P.82–83, POCKET MAP E2

Classic Malasaña café and a
great place to while away an
afternoon. Discreet background
music and good cakes are
followed by cocktails in the
evening.

CAFÉ LA PALMA

C/Palma 62 Ⓜ Noviciado Ⓦ www.cafe
lapalma.com. Daily 4pm–3am. MAP P.82–83,
POCKET MAP D2

Part traditional café, part arts
and music venue, *Café La
Palma* acts as a venue for a
myriad of local artists ranging
from singer-songwriters to
storytellers. It also has popular
DJ sessions on many evenings.

Restaurants

LA BARRACA

C/Reina 29 Ⓜ Bilbao ☎ 915 327 154.
Daily 1.30–4.30pm & 8.30pm–midnight.
MAP P.82–83, POCKET MAP F4

Step off the dingy street into
this little piece of Valencia for
some of the best *paella* in town.
The starters are excellent and
there's a great lemon sorbet
for dessert too. A three-course
meal with wine costs around
€35 a head.

BAZAAR

C/Libertad 21 Ⓜ Chueca. Mon–Wed &
Sun 1.15–4pm & 8.30–11.30pm, Thurs–Sat
1.15–4pm & 8.15pm–midnight. MAP P.82–83,
POCKET MAP G4

Fusion-style Mediterranean
and Asian cuisine. Lunchtime
menu is just €10; evening meals
for around €20. The down side
is the production-line-style
service. No reservations, so
arrive early.

CAFÉ OLIVER

C/Almirante 12 Ⓜ Chueca ☎ 915 217 379.
Mon–Sat 1.30–4.30pm & 9pm–midnight,
Sun 11.30am–4pm. MAP P.82–83, POCKET
MAP G3

Stylish surroundings and food
in this trendy bistro. There's
a €14 lunchtime menu with
dishes such as peppers stuffed
with hake and seafood pasta,
while the €25 Sunday brunch
is very popular if rather
overpriced.

EL COMUNISTA (TIENDA DE VINOS)

C/Augusto Figueroa 35 Ⓜ Chueca
☎ 915 217 012. Mon–Sat 1–4.30pm &
9.30–11.45pm, Sun 9.30–11.45pm.
Closed mid-Aug to mid-Sept. MAP P.82–83,
POCKET MAP G4

Long-established *comedor* that
has changed little since it was
given its unofficial name as a
student haunt under Franco.
The *sopa de ajo* (garlic soup)
is delicious.

DIVINA LA COCINA

C/Colmenares 13 Ⓜ Chueca ☎ 915 313 765.
Mon–Sun 1–4pm & 9pm–midnight (open till
1am on Sat & Sun). MAP P.82–83, POCKET MAP G4

Fashionable restaurant on a

little street close to Gran Vía. Lunch menus from €13.90; the evening menu is more expensive (around €26). Dishes include stuffed courgettes, ostrich burgers and superb cheesecakes.

LA GLORIA DE MONTERA

C/Caballero de Gracia 10 Ⓜ Gran Vía. Daily 1–4pm & 8.30–11.45pm. MAP P.82–83, POCKET MAP F10

Cool and airy sister restaurant to *La Finca de Susana* (see p.60). *Menú* at €10 with well-presented dishes. No reservations.

MOMO

C/Libertad 8 Ⓜ Chueca ☎ 915 327 348. Daily 1–4pm & 9.30pm–midnight. MAP P.82–83, POCKET MAP G4

The place to go for a *menú del día* with a little bit extra. For €16.50 you get three courses, with options such as chicken kebabs marinated in coriander or duck with caramelized pears. Unusually, they also do a set dinner in the evening for €18.50.

MONONOKE

C/Hernán Cortés 19 Ⓜ Chueca ☎ 915 229 806. Mon–Sat 1.30–4pm & 8.30pm–midnight. MAP P.82–83, POCKET MAP F3

Very friendly staff in this small Japanese restaurant in the heart of Chueca. Great value with a selection of sushi, sashimi, tempura and tori teriyaki menus all available for around €20.

LA MUSA

C/Manuela Malasaña 18 Ⓜ Bilbao ☎ 914 487 558. Mon–Fri 9am–midnight, Sat 1pm–2am, Sun 1pm–midnight. MAP P.82–83, POCKET MAP E1

A firm favourite on the Malasaña scene. Good tapas, generous helpings, strong wine list and chic decor are all part of the recipe for success. The only problem is the crowds.

RIBEIRA DO MIÑO

C/Santa Brígida 1 Ⓜ Tribunal ☎ 915 219 854. Tues–Sun 1–5pm & 8pm–midnight. MAP P.82–83, POCKET MAP F3

Great-value *marisquería*, serving fabulous seafood platters and Galician specialities at great prices; try the slightly more expensive Galician white wine, Albariño. Reservations essential.

SALVADOR

C/Barbieri 12 Ⓜ Chueca ☎ 915 214 524. Mon–Sat 1.30–4pm & 9pm–midnight. Closed Aug. MAP P.82–83, POCKET MAP G4

Chueca mainstay with bullfighting decor and dishes such as *rabo de toro* (bull's tail), *gallina en pepitoria* (chicken in almond sauce) and *arroz con leche* (rice pudding). Lunch around €20.

LA BARRACA

GRAN VÍA, CHUECA AND MALASAÑA

Tapas bars

ALBUR

C/Manuela Malasaña 15 Ⓜ Bilbao.
Daily noon–1am (2am Fri & Sat). MAP P.82–83,
POCKET MAP E1

The decor is rustic and the food excellent here, but the service is a little slow. The salads and the cheese platters are excellent, as is the grilled octopus. The lunchtime menu is €11.50.

BACO Y BETO

C/Pelayo 24 Ⓜ Chueca. Mon–Fri 8pm–1am,
Sat 2–4pm & 8pm–1am. MAP P.82–83, POCKET
MAP F3

Creative tapas in this small bar in the heart of Chueca. Try the sirloin canapé soaked in bitter orange and the home-made *croquetas*.

EL BOCAITO

C/Libertad 6 Ⓜ Chueca. Mon–Fri 1–4.30pm
& 8.30pm–midnight, Sat 8.30pm–midnight.
Closed Aug. MAP P.82–83, POCKET MAP G4

Watch the busy staff preparing the food in the kitchen as you munch on delicious tapas. Try the *Luisito* (chilli, squid and a secret sauce all topped with a prawn), the hottest canapé you're ever likely to encounter. If you prefer to sit down, there is a restaurant at the back.

GOURMET EXPERIENCE

El Corte Inglés, Plaza Callao 2 Ⓜ Callao.
Mon–Sat 10am–midnight. MAP P.82–83, POCKET
MAP D10

Head for the ninth floor of this branch of the classic Spanish department store to enjoy some breathtaking views of Madrid. Gaze out over the Capitol building on the Gran Vía, the Palacio Real, and out towards the distant mountains as you sample a tapa, some oysters, a drink or an ice cream from one of the bars and food stalls set up on the top floor.

MERCADO DE SAN ANTÓN

C/Augusto Figueroa 24 Ⓜ Chueca. Mon–
Sat 10am–10pm, terrace and restaurant
Mon–Thurs & Sun 10am–midnight, Fri & Sat
10am–1.30am. MAP P.82–83, POCKET MAP G4

Like the Mercado San Miguel near Plaza Mayor, this local market has become a trendy meeting place on the Chueca scene with gourmet foodstands, a wine bar, a café, a sushi stall and a stylish terrace restaurant.

STOP MADRID

C/Hortaleza 11 Ⓜ Gran Vía. Daily noon–2am.
MAP P.82–83, POCKET MAP F4

Dating back to 1929, this corner bar has hams hanging from the windows and wine bottles lining the walls. Tapas consist largely of *jamón* and *chorizo*, and the "Canapé Stop" of ham and tomato doused in olive oil is an excellent option.

Bars

LA ARDOSA

C/Colón 13 Ⓜ Tribunal. Daily 8.30–2am. MAP
P.82–83, POCKET MAP F3

One of the city's classic tabernas, serving limited but delicious tapas including great *croquetas*, *salmorejo* and an excellent home-made *tortilla*. Also draft beer and Guinness.

CHICOTE

Gran Vía 12 Ⓜ Gran Vía. Mon–Sat
5pm–1.30am. MAP P.82–83, POCKET MAP F10

Opened back in 1931 by Perico Chicote, ex-barman at the *Ritz*. Sophia Loren, Frank Sinatra, Ava Gardner, Luis Buñuel, Orson Welles and Hemingway have all passed through the doors of this cocktail bar. It's lost much of its old-style charm as it has tried to keep up to date, though it's still worth a visit for nostalgia's sake.

DEL DIEGO

C/Reina 12 Ⓜ Gran Vía. Mon–Sat 9pm–3am. Closed Aug. MAP P.82–83, POCKET, MAP F10

New York-style cocktail bar set up by former *Chicote* waiter Fernando del Diego and now better than the original place. The expertly mixed cocktails are served up in a friendly, unhurried atmosphere. Margaritas, mojitos and manhattans; the eponymously named vodka-based house special is a must.

FINNEGANS

Plaza de Las Salesas 9 Ⓜ Alonso Martinez. Daily 8am–2am. MAP P.82–83, POCKET MAP G3

Irish bar with several rooms, complete with bar fittings and wooden floors brought over from the Emerald Isle. English-speaking staff and live Premier League football and international rugby on TV.

GIN CLUB/MERCADO DE LA REINA

Gran Vía 12 Ⓜ Gran Vía. Gin Club 1.30pm–late, bar & tapas: 9am–midnight (Fri & Sat 1am), restaurant: 1.30–4pm & 8.30pm–midnight. MAP P.82–83, POCKET MAP G10 & F10

A tapas bar, restaurant and *bar de copas*. The bar serves a wide range of *pinchos* and *raciones* as well as a house special (upmarket) hamburger meal at €10.50. The restaurant is rather more pricey, with main courses around €15. At the back, with its mirrored ceilings and black leather chairs, is the *Gin Club* cocktail bar, offering over twenty different brands.

PEPE BOTELLA

C/San Andrés 12 Ⓜ Bilbao. Daily 11am–2am. MAP P.82–83, POCKET MAP E2

Elegant little bar perched on the edge of the Plaza Dos de Mayo. Friendly staff, marble-topped tables, low-volume music and no fruit machine.

TABERNA ÁNGEL SIERRA

C/Gravina 11 Ⓜ Chueca. Daily noon–1am. MAP P.82–83, POCKET MAP G3

One of the great bars in Madrid, where everyone drinks *vermút* accompanied by free, exquisite pickled anchovy tapas. *Raciones* are also available in the seated area, though they are a little pricey.

Clubs

OHM/WEEKEND AT BASH

Plaza Callao 4 Ⓜ Callao Ⓦ www.tripfamily.com. Wed 11pm–6am, Thurs–Sat midnight–6am, Sun midnight–5am. €12–15, including first drink. MAP P.82–83, POCKET MAP D4

OHM is the main techno/house session on Fridays and popular with the gay crowd. Wednesday is funk/hip hop, with Thursday more electro. *Weekend* is the Saturday session.

TEATRO BARCELÓ

C/Barceló 11 Ⓜ Tribunal. Wed–Sat midnight–5am. €15 with drink. MAP P.82–83, POCKET MAP F2

Formerly known as *Pachá*, this club, housed in a fantastic Art Deco building, runs an early session for under-age clubbers 6.30–10.30pm on Fridays and Saturdays and then gets going with the real thing from midnight. House and techno on Saturdays; the music is more varied on other nights.

TUPPERWARE

C/Corredera Alta de San Pablo 26 Ⓜ Tribunal. Daily 9pm–3.30am. MAP P.82–83, POCKET MAP F2

A Malasaña legend with retro decor and reasonably priced drinks, this is the place to go for indie tunes, with grunge and punk era classics. Downstairs is usually packed to the rafters, but upstairs the atmosphere is more relaxed.

Salamanca and Paseo de la Castellana

Exclusive Barrio de Salamanca was developed in the second half of the nineteenth century as an upmarket residential zone under the patronage of the Marquis of Salamanca. Today it's still home to Madrid's smartest apartments and designer emporiums, while the streets are populated by the chic clothes and sunglasses brigade, decked out in fur coats, Gucci and gold. Shopping aside, there's a scattering of sights here, including the pick of the city's smaller museums and Real Madrid's imposing Santiago Bernabéu stadium. Bordering Salamanca to the west is the multi-lane Paseo de la Castellana, peppered with corporate office blocks, where, in summer, the section north of Plaza de Colón is littered with trendy *terrazas*.

PLAZA DE COLÓN

Ⓜ Colón. MAP P.92, POCKET MAP H3

Overlooking a busy crossroads and dominating the square in which they stand are a Neo-Gothic monument to Christopher Columbus (Cristóbal Colón), given as a wedding gift to Alfonso XII, and an enormous Spanish flag. Directly behind are the Jardines del Descubrimiento (Discovery Gardens), a small park containing three huge stone blocks representing Columbus's ships, the *Niña*, *Pinta* and *Santa María*. Below the plaza, underneath a cascading wall of water, is the **Teatro Fernán Gómez**, a venue for theatre, film, dance, music and occasional exhibitions.

BIBLIOTECA NACIONAL AND MUSEO DEL LIBRO

Paseo de Recoletos 20 Ⓜ Colón Ⓦ www .bne.es. Tues–Sat 10am–9pm, Sun & hols 10am–2pm. Free. MAP P.92, POCKET MAP J3

The National Library contains over six million volumes, including every work published in Spain since 1716. The museum within displays a selection of the library's treasures, including Arab, Hebrew and Greek manuscripts, and hosts regular temporary exhibitions related to the world of art and literature.

MUSEO ARQUEOLÓGICO NACIONAL

C/Serrano 13 Ⓜ Serrano or Colón Ⓦ man .mcu.es. Tues–Sat 9.30am–8pm, Sun 9.30am–3pm. Check website for entrance fees. MAP P.92, POCKET MAP J3

Due for a 2014 reopening after a long overdue restoration programme, the archeological museum's vast collections trace the cultural evolution of humankind. Most exhibits are from Spain and include striking **Celto-Iberian busts** known as *La Dama de Elche* and *La Dama de Baza*. There are some suitably enigmatic sphinx-like sculptures found in Alicante and a wonderfully rich hoard of Visigothic treasures found at Toledo. Good coverage is also given to Roman, Egyptian, Greek and Islamic finds.

MUSEO DE CERA

Paseo de Recoletos 41 Ⓜ Colón Ⓦ www.museoceramadrid.com. Mon–Fri 10am–2.30pm & 4.30–8.30pm, Sat, Sun & hols 10am–8.30pm. €17 (€12 for 4–12 year olds). MAP P.92, POCKET MAP H3

Over 450 different personalities – including a host of VIPs, heads of state and, of course,

Real Madrid football stars – are displayed in this expensive and tacky museum, which is nevertheless popular with children. There's also a chamber of horrors and a film history of Spain (supplement charged).

MUSEO DE ARTE PÚBLICO

Paseo de la Castellana 41 Ⓜ Rubén Darío. MAP P.92, POCKET MAP J1

An innovative use of the space underneath the Juan Bravo flyover, this open-air art museum is made up of a haphazard collection of sculptures, cubes, walls and fountains, including work by Eduardo Chillida, Joan Miró and Julio González.

MUSEO SOROLLA

Paseo del General Martínez Campos 37 Ⓜ Rubén Darío, Gregorio Marañon or Iglesia Ⓦ museosorolla.mcu.es. Tues–Sat 9.30am–8pm, Sun 10am–3pm. €3, free Sat 2–8pm & Sun. MAP P.92, POCKET MAP J1

Part museum and part art gallery, this tribute to an artist's life and work is one of Madrid's most underrated treasures. Situated in Joaquín Sorolla's former home, it's a delightful oasis of peace and tranquillity, its cool and shady Andalusian-style courtyard and gardens decked out with statues, fountains, assorted plants and fruit trees. The ground floor has been kept largely intact, re-creating the authentic atmosphere of the artist's living and working areas. The upstairs rooms, originally the sleeping quarters, have been turned into a gallery, where sunlight, sea, intense colours, women and children dominate Sorolla's impressionistic paintings. On your way out in the Patio Andaluz, there's a collection of his sketches and gouaches.

Salamanca and Paseo de la Castellana

ACCOMMODATION
Hostal Residencia Don Diego	5
Hotel Orfila	4
Hotel Santo Mauro	1
Hotel Unico	2
Petit Palace Embassy	3

SHOPPING
ABC Serrano	2
Adolfo Domínguez	6
Area Real Madrid	1
Agatha Ruiz de la Prada	4
Ekseptión	5
Lavinia	3

CAFÉS
Café el Espejo	12
Café Gijón	14

RESTAURANTS
Estay	11
Hard Rock Café	10
El Pescador	5
Ramón Freixa Madrid	7
Sergi Arola Gastro	4

TAPAS BARS
Hevia	2
Lateral	1, 3, 6

BARS
Le Cabrera	13
Castellana 8	8
Teatriz	9

CLUBS
Moma 56	1
Serrano 41	2

MUSEO LÁZARO GALDIANO

C/Serrano 122 Ⓜ Gregorio Marañon Ⓦ www
.flg.es. Mon & Wed-Sat 10am–4.30pm,
Sun 10am–3pm. €6, free 3.30–4.30pm, Sun
2–3pm. MAP P.92, POCKET MAP J1

When businessman and
publisher José Lázaro Galdiano
died in 1947, he left his private
collection – a vast treasure trove
of paintings and *objets d'art* – to
the state. Spread over the four
floors of his former home, the
collection contains jewellery,
outstanding Spanish archeological pieces and some beautifully
decorated thirteenth-century
Limoges enamels. There's
also an excellent selection of
European paintings with works
by Bosch, Rembrandt, Reynolds
and Constable, plus Spanish
artists including Zurbarán,
Velázquez, El Greco and Goya.
Other exhibits include several
clocks and watches, many of
them once owned by Emperor
Charles V.

MUSEO DE CIENCIAS NATURALES

C/José Gutiérrez Abascal 2 Ⓜ Gregorio
Marañon Ⓦ www.mncn.csic.es. Tues–Fri, Sun
& hols 10am–5pm, Sat 10am–8pm (July &
Aug 10am–3pm). €6. MAP P.92, POCKET MAP J1

The Natural History Museum's
displays are split between two
buildings. One contains a fairly
predictable collection of stuffed
animals, skeletons and audio-
visual displays on the evolution
of life on earth, the other is
home to some rather dull fossil
and geological exhibits.

ESTADIO SANTIAGO BERNABÉU

C/Concha Espina 1 Ⓜ Santiago Bernabéu
☎ 913 984 300, tickets ☎ 902 324 324,
Ⓦ www.realmadrid.com. Ticket office
daily 10–7pm (match days from 11am).
Tickets from €30. Tour and trophy exhibition:
Mon–Sat 10am–7pm, Sun 10.30am–6.30pm
(closes five hours before games on
match days); €19, under-14s €13. MAP P.92,
POCKET MAP J1

The magnificent 80,000-seater
Bernabéu stadium provides a
suitably imposing home for
one of the most glamorous
teams in football, Real Madrid.
Venue of the 1982 World Cup
final, the stadium has witnessed
countless triumphs of "Los
blancos", who have notched up
32 Spanish league titles and
nine European Cup triumphs
in their 111-year history. Real
have broken the world transfer
record three times in the last
decade, and their latest star
is Portugal forward Cristiano
Ronaldo. Tickets for big games
can be tricky to get hold of,
but the club runs a telephone
and internet booking service
(see opposite).

You can catch a glimpse of
the hallowed turf on the over-
priced stadium tour during
which you visit the changing
rooms, walk around the edge of
the pitch and sit in the VIP box
before heading to the trophy
room with its endless cabinets
of gleaming silverware. The
stadium also has a reasonably
priced café (*Realcafé*) and two
more expensive restaurants
(*Puerta 57* and *Asador de la
Esquina*) both open to the
public and affording views over
the pitch (though they are not
open during games).

TROPHIES AT ESTADIO SANTIAGO BERNABÉU

PLAZA DE TOROS DE LAS VENTAS

PLAZA CASTILLA

Ⓜ Plaza de la Castilla. MAP P.92, POCKET MAP J1

The Paseo de la Castellana ends with a flourish at Plaza Castilla with the dramatic leaning towers of the Puerta de Europa and the four giant skyscrapers constructed on Real Madrid's former training ground, the result of a controversial deal that allowed the club to solve many of its financial problems. The two tallest towers – one designed by Norman Foster – soar some 250 metres skywards.

PLAZA DE TOROS DE LAS VENTAS

C/Alcalá 237 Ⓜ Ventas ☎ 913 562 200, Ⓦ www.las-ventas.com. Box office March–Oct Thurs–Sun 10am–2pm & 4–7pm; ☎ 902 150 025, Ⓦ www.taquilatoros.com. €5–150. MAP P.92

On the easternmost tip of the Barrio de Salamanca, Madrid's 23,000-capacity, Neo-Mudéjar bullring, Las Ventas, is the most illustrious in the world. The season lasts from March to October and *corridas* (bullfights) are held every Sunday at 7pm and every day during the three main *ferias* (fairs): La Comunidad (early May), San Isidro (mid-May to June) and Otoño (late Sept to Oct). Tickets go on sale at the ring a couple of days in advance, though many are already allocated to season-ticket holders. The cheapest seats are *gradas*, the highest rows at the back, from where you can see everything that happens without too much detail; the front rows are known as the *barreras*. Seats are also divided into *sol* (sun), *sombra* (shade) and *sol y sombra* (shaded after a while), with *sombra* the most expensive.

There's a taurine **museum** attached to the bullring (March–Oct Tues–Fri 9.30am–2.30pm, Sun & fight days 10am–1pm; Nov–Feb Mon–Fri 9.30am–2pm; free) with an intriguing collection of bullfighting memorabilia including stunning *trajes de luces*, the beautifully decorated suits worn by the *toreros*. You can also step onto the sand yourself with a tour of the bullring (daily 10am–6pm, 10am–2pm on *corrida* days; €10 with audioguide).

Shops

ABC SERRANO

Paseo de la Castellana 34 and C/Serrano 61 both Ⓜ Rubén Darío. Mon–Sat 9.15am–9pm, Sun noon–8pm. MAP P.92, POCKET MAP J1

Upmarket shopping mall housed in the beautiful former headquarters of the **ABC** newspaper. There are fashion and household outlets, as well as a couple of bars and restaurants, and a popular rooftop terrace.

ADOLFO DOMÍNGUEZ

C/Serrano 3 Ⓜ Retiro. Mon–Sat 10am–8.30pm. MAP P.92, POCKET MAP J4

Domínguez has opened a

massive five-storey flagship store for his slightly sober but elegant modern Spanish designs – a wide range of natural colours and free lines for both men and women.

AREA REAL MADRID

Bernabéu Stadium; C/Padre Damián, Puerta 55 Ⓜ Santiago Bernabéu. Daily 10.30am–8.30pm. MAP P.92, POCKET MAP J1

Club store where you can pick up all manner of rather expensive souvenirs related to the club's history and replica shirts of the star players.

AGATHA RUIZ DE LA PRADA

C/Serrano 27 Ⓜ Serrano. Mon–Sat 10am–8.30pm. MAP P.92, POCKET MAP J2

Movida-era designer who shows and sells her gaudily coloured clothes and accessories at this dazzling outlet. There's a children's line, stationery and household goods too.

EKSEPTIÓN

C/Velázquez 28 Ⓜ Velázquez. Mon–Sat 10.30am–8.30pm. MAP P.92, POCKET MAP K3

A dramatic catwalk bathed in spotlights leads into this shop selling some of the most expensive women's clothes in Madrid. Next door are younger, more casual clothes in the Eks shop for both men and women. There's also a branch selling discount last-season fashions at half-price at Avenida Concha Espina 14 (Mon–Sat 11am–7pm).

LAVINIA

C/José Ortega y Gasset 16 Ⓜ Nuñez de Balboa. Mon–Sat 10am–9pm. MAP P.92, POCKET MAP K1

A massive wine shop with a great selection from Spain and the rest of the world. The perfect place to get that Ribera del Duero, Albariño or Rueda that you wanted to take home.

Cafés

CAFÉ EL ESPEJO

Paseo de Recoletos 31 Ⓜ Colón. Daily 8am–1am. MAP P.92, POCKET MAP H3

Opened in 1978, but you really wouldn't guess it from the antiquated decor – think mirrors, gilt and a wonderful, extravagant glass pavilion. The leafy outside *terraza* is an ideal spot to enjoy a coffee and watch the world go by.

CAFÉ GIJÓN

Paseo de Recoletos 21 Ⓜ Colón. Daily 8am–1.30am. MAP P.92, POCKET MAP H4

A famous literary café dating from 1888, decked out in Cuban mahogany and mirrors. A centre of the *Movida* in the 1980s, it still hosts regular artistic *tertulias* (discussion groups). There's a cellar restaurant, but you're best off sticking to drinks in the bar or on the pleasant summer *terraza*.

AGATHA RUIZ DE LA PRADA

CAFÉ EL ESPEJO

Restaurants

ESTAY

C/Hermosilla 46 Ⓜ Velázquez
☎ 915 780 470, Mon–Sat 1–4pm &
8pm–midnight. MAP P.92, POCKET MAP K2

Basque-style cuisine in minia-ture (canapés and mini casse-roles) in this pleasant, roomy restaurant. A great range of *pintxos*, including *jamón* with roquefort cheese, langoustine vol-au-vents and a fine wine list too. A meal will cost €25–30.

HARD ROCK CAFÉ

Paseo de la Castellana 2 Ⓜ Colón
☎ 914 364 340. Daily 12.30pm–2am.
MAP P.92, POCKET MAP J2

A children's favourite, with its tried-and-tested formula of rock memorabilia, Tex-Mex and burgers at under €20 a head. The best thing about it is the summer *terraza* overlooking Plaza Colón.

EL PESCADOR

C/José Ortega y Gasset 75 Ⓜ Lista
☎ 914 021 290. Mon–Sat 12.30–4pm &
7.30pm–midnight. Closed Aug. MAP P.92,
POCKET MAP K1

One of the city's top seafood restaurants, with specials flown in daily from the Atlantic. Prices are high (around €55 per head), but you'll rarely experi-ence better-quality seafood

than this. If funds don't stretch to a full meal, you can try a *ración* in the bar instead.

RAMÓN FREIXA MADRID

C/Claudio Coello 67 Ⓜ Serrano
☎ 917 818 262. Tues–Sat 1–4pm &
8.30–midnight. MAP P.92, POCKET MAP J2

Catalan chef Ramón Freixa's flagship Michelin-starred restaurant in Madrid situated in the luxury surroundings of the *Hotel Único* (see p.129) in the heart of Salamanca. Creative and impeccably presented dishes from an ever-changing menu featuring superb game, fish and new twists on Spanish classics. A la carte dishes range €25–55, while there is a selec-tion of taster menus available from €75. Only has space for 35 diners, so book well in advance, especially if you want a table in the summer terrace.

SERGI AROLA GASTRO

C/Zurbano 31 Ⓜ Rubén Darío ☎ 913 102
169 ⓦ sergiarola.es. Tues–Sat 2–3.30pm &
9–11.30pm. Closed Easter and two weeks in
Aug. MAP P.92, POCKET MAP H1

Former pupil of Spanish chef extraordinaire Ferran Adrià, Arola launched this intimate showcase for his innovative cuisine with his wife Sara Fort. The seasonal menus display an inspired range of fresh produce, with set menus ranging from

€105–€135, though there is also a €45 weekday lunchtime menu and a children's option (under-14s) for €25 at Saturday lunch. If you go a la carte expect to pay €50 for creations such as roast venison and hare with apple and black truffle sauce.

Tapas bars

HEVIA

C/Serrano 118 Ⓜ Rubén Darío or Gregorio Marañon. Mon–Sat 9am–1.30am. MAP P.92, POCKET MAP J1

Plush venue for plush clientele feasting on pricey but excellent tapas and canapés – the hot Camembert is delicious, as is the *surtido de ahumados* (selection of smoked fish).

LATERAL

Paseo de la Castellana 42 Ⓜ Rubén Darío. Daily 10am–midnight. MAP P.92, POCKET MAP J1

A swish tapas bar serving classic dishes such as *croquetas* and *pimientos rellenos* (stuffed peppers) with a modern twist. It's close to the Bernabéu and gets crowded on match days but there are other branches at C/Velázquez 57, C/Fuencarral 43, Paseo de la Castellana 89 and Plaza Santa Ana 12.

Bars

CASTELLANA 8

Paseo de la Castellana 8 Ⓜ Colón. Mon–Fri 1pm–3am, Sat & Sun 8pm–3am. MAP P.92, POCKET MAP J2

Restaurant and café by day, cocktail bar and club by night, *Castellana 8* has a laidback atmosphere, cool decor and a terrace perfect for chilling out on a hot summer evening.

TEATRIZ

C/Hermosilla 15 Ⓜ Serrano. Bar 9pm–3am, restaurant 1.30–4.30pm & 9pm–1am; closed Sat lunch, Sun & Aug. MAP P.92, POCKET MAP J2

This former theatre was stylishly refurbished by Catalan designer Javier Mariscal and Frenchman Philippe Starck. There's a tapas bar at the entrance, a bar on the stage and a restaurant in the stalls. Sip the pricey drinks slowly, savouring your surroundings.

Clubs

MOMA 56

C/José Abascal 56 Ⓜ Gregorio Marañon Ⓦ www.moma56.com. Wed–Sun midnight–6am. Around €15. MAP P.92, POCKET MAP J1

An exclusive club, popular with *pijos* (rich kids) and the upmarket glamour crowd. Also inside are a restaurant and a bar serving cocktails and light Mediterranean fusion food.

SERRANO 41

C/Serrano 41 Ⓜ Serrano Ⓦ serrano41.com. Wed–Sun midnight–5.30am. Around €12. MAP P.92, POCKET MAP J1

Plush, two-floored disco in the heart of Salamanca, popular with *pijos* and footballers and complete with VIP zone, chill-out areas and a summer terrace. Music ranges from pop and house to funk and hip-hop.

RAMON FREIXA MADRID

Plaza de España and beyond

Largely constructed in the Franco era and dominated by two early Spanish skyscrapers, the Plaza de España provides an imposing full stop to Gran Vía and a breathing space from the densely packed streets to the east. Beyond the square lies a mixture of aristocratic suburbia, university campus and parkland, distinguished by the green swathes of Parque del Oeste and Casa de Campo. Sights include the eclectic collections of the Museo Cerralbo, the fascinating Museo de América, the Ermita de San Antonio de la Florida, with its stunning Goya frescoes and, further out, the pleasant royal residence of El Pardo. Meanwhile, the spacious *terrazas* along Paseo del Pintor Rosales provide ample opportunity for refreshment.

PLAZA DE ESPAÑA

Ⓜ Plaza de España. MAP P.100, POCKET MAP C3

The Plaza de España was the Spanish dictator Franco's attempt to portray Spain as a dynamic, modern country. The gargantuan apartment complex of the **Edificio de España**, which heads the square, looks like it was transplanted from 1920s New York, but was in fact completed in 1953. Four years later, the 32-storey **Torre de Madrid** took over for some time as the tallest building in Spain. Together they tower over an elaborate monument to Cervantes in the middle of the square, set by an uninspiring pool. The plaza itself can be a little seedy at night, although it does play

DON QUIXOTE IN PLAZA ESPAÑA

host to occasional festivities and an interesting craft fair during the fiesta of San Isidro (on or around May 15).

MUSEO DE CERRALBO

C/Ventura Rodríguez 17 Ⓜ Plaza de España Ⓦ museocerralbo.mcu.es. Tues, Wed, Fri & Sat 9.30am–3pm, plus Thurs 5–8pm, Sun & hols 10am–3pm. €3, free Sat after 2pm & Sun. MAP P.100, POCKET MAP B3

Reactionary politician, poet, traveller and archeologist, the seventeenth Marqués de Cerralbo endowed his elegant nineteenth-century mansion with a substantial collection of paintings, furniture and armour. Bequeathed to the state on his death, the house opened as a museum in 1962 and the cluttered nature of the exhibits is partly explained by the fact that the marqués's will stipulated that objects should be displayed exactly as he had arranged them. The highlight is a fabulous over-the-top mirrored ballroom with a Tiepolo-inspired fresco, golden stuccowork and marbled decoration.

CENTRO CULTURAL CONDE DUQUE

C/Conde Duque 9–11 Ⓜ Ventura Rodríguez Ⓦ www.esmadrid.com/condeduque. MAP P.100, POCKET MAP C2

Constructed in the early eighteenth century, this former royal guard barracks has been converted into a dynamic cultural centre, housing the city's **contemporary art** collection and hosting a variety of exhibitions and concerts.

PLAZA DE COMENDADORAS

Ⓜ Noviciado. MAP P.100, POCKET MAP D2

Bordered by a variety of interesting craft shops, bars and cafés, this tranquil square is named after the convent that occupies one side of it. The convent is run by nuns from the military order of Santiago and the attached church is decked out with banners celebrating the victories of the Order's knights. A large painting of their patron, St James the Moor-slayer, hangs over the high altar. The plaza itself comes alive in the summer months when the *terrazas* open and locals gather for a chat and a drink.

Plaza de España and beyond

| | metres | 250 |
| | yards | 250 |

ACCOMMODATION
Casón del Tormes	3
Hostal Buenos Aires	2
Hotel Emperador	4
Hotel Santo Domingo	5
Hotel Tirol	1

SHOPPING
El Corte Inglés	1
Ocho y Medio	3
Santmery	2

CLUB
Galileo Galilei	1

BAR
El Jardín Secreto	7

CAFÉ
Café Moderno	4

RESTAURANTS
Café del Oriente	1
Casa Mingo	8
La Taberna de Liria	6
Toma	5
Urogallo	9
La Vaca Argentina	3

TAPAS BAR
Casa Paco	2

PLAZA DE COMENDADORAS

Nov–April Tues–Sat 9.30am–6.30pm, Sun 10am–3pm. €3, free Sun. MAP P.100, POCKET MAP B1

This fabulous collection of pre-Columbian American art and artefacts includes objects brought back at the time of the Spanish Conquest, as well as more recent acquisitions and donations. The layout is thematic, with sections on geography, history, social organization, religion and communication. The Aztec, Maya and Inca civilizations are well represented and exhibits include: the Madrid Codex, one of only three surviving hieroglyphic manuscripts depicting everyday Maya life; the Tudela Codex, with indigenous paintings describing the events of the Spanish Conquest; and the Quimbayas Treasure, a breathtaking collection of gold objects from a funeral treasure of the Colombian Quimbaya culture, dated 900–600 BC.

MINISTERIO DEL AIRE

Ⓜ Moncloa. MAP P.100, POCKET MAP B1

The Air Ministry is a product of the post-Civil War Francoist building boom. Work on the mammoth edifice began in 1942, and even the Third Reich's architect, Albert Speer, was consulted. However, with the defeat of the Nazis, plans were soon changed and a Habsburg-style structure was built instead – nicknamed the "Monasterio" del Aire because of its similarity to El Escorial. The neighbouring Arco de la Victoria was constructed in 1956 to commemorate the Nationalist military triumph in the Civil War.

MUSEO DE AMÉRICA

Avda de los Reyes Católicos 6 Ⓜ Moncloa Ⓦ museodeamerica.mcu.es. May–Oct Tues–Sat 9.30am–8.30pm, Sun 10am–3pm;

MUSEO DE AMÉRICA

MUSEO DEL TRAJE

Avda de Juan de Herrera 2 Ⓜ Moncloa
Ⓦ museodeltraje.mcu.es. Tues–Sat
9.30am–7pm, Sun & hols 10am–3pm (July
& Aug open late from 9.30am–10.30pm on
Thurs). €3, free Sat after 2.30pm and all day
Sun. MAP P.100, POCKET MAP B1

A fascinating excursion through the history of clothes and costume. Exhibits include garments from a royal tomb dating back to the thirteenth century, some stunning eighteenth-century ballgowns and a selection of Spanish regional costumes as well as shoes, jewellery and underwear. Modern Spanish and international designers are also featured, with a Paco Rabane mini-skirt and elegant shoes from Pedro del Hierro. There is an upmarket restaurant in the grounds, which has a cool garden terrace in the summer (see p.106).

PARQUE DEL OESTE

Ⓜ Moncloa. MAP P.100, POCKET MAP A3

Featuring a pleasant stream, assorted statues and shady walks, this delightful park offers a welcome respite from the busy streets of the capital. In summer there are numerous *terrazas* overlooking it on Paseo del Pintor Rosales. The beautiful rose garden – in C/Rosaleda – is at its most fragrant in May and June, while further down the hill is a small cemetery where the 43 Spaniards executed by occupying French troops on May 3, 1808 – and immortalized by Goya in his famous painting in the Prado (see p.66) – lie buried.

TEMPLO DE DEBOD

C/Ferraz 1 Ⓜ Plaza de España. April–Sept
Tues–Fri 10am–2pm & 6–8pm, Sat &
Sun 9.30am–8pm; Oct–March Tues–Fri
9.45am–1.45pm & 4.15–6.15pm, Sat & Sun
9.30am–8pm. Free. MAP P.100, POCKET MAP B3

A fourth-century BC Egyptian temple in the middle of Madrid may seem an incongruous sight. It's here, however, as a thank-you from the Egyptian government for Spanish help in salvaging archeological sites threatened by the construction of the Aswan High Dam. Reconstructed here stone by stone in 1968, it has a multimedia exhibition on the culture of Ancient Egypt inside. Archeologists have called for it to be enclosed and insulated from the open air as pollution is taking a heavy toll on the stone.

EL TELEFÉRICO

CASA DE CAMPO

EL TELEFÉRICO

Paseo del Pintor Rosales Ⓜ Argüelles Ⓦ www.teleferico.com. April–Sept Mon–Fri noon–early eve (exact times vary), Sat & Sun noon–around 8pm; Oct–March Sat, Sun & hols noon–dusk. €4 single, €5.75 return. MAP P.100, POCKET MAP A2

The Teleférico **cable car** shuttles passengers from the edge of the Parque del Oeste high over the Manzanares river to a restaurant/bar in the middle of Casa de Campo (see below). The round trip offers some fine views of the park, the Palacio Real, the Almudena Cathedral and the city skyline.

LA ERMITA DE SAN ANTONIO DE LA FLORIDA

Paseo de la Florida 5 Ⓜ Príncipe Pío Ⓦ www .munimadrid.es/ermita. Tues–Sun 9.30am–8pm. Free. MAP P.100, POCKET MAP A4

Built on a Greek-cross plan between 1792 and 1798, this little church is the burial site of Goya and also features some outstanding frescoes by him. Those in the dome depict St Anthony of Padua resurrecting a dead man to give evidence in favour of a prisoner (the saint's father) unjustly accused of murder. The *ermita* also houses the artist's mausoleum, although his head was stolen by phrenologists for examination in the nineteenth century. The

mirror-image chapel on the other side of the road was built in 1925 for parish services so that the original could become a museum. On St Anthony's Day (June 13) girls queue at the church to ask the saint for a boyfriend; if pins dropped into the holy water then stick to their hands, their wish will be granted.

CASA DE CAMPO

Ⓜ Lago. MAP P.100, POCKET MAP A4

The Casa de Campo, an enormous expanse of heath and scrub, is in parts surprisingly wild for a place so easily accessible from the city. Founded by Felipe II in the mid-sixteenth century as a royal hunting estate, it was only opened to the public in 1931 and soon after acted as a base for Franco's forces to shell the city. Large sections have been tamed for conventional pastimes and there are picnic tables and café/ bars throughout the park, the ones by the lake providing fine views of the city. There are also mountain-bike trails, a jogging track, an open-air swimming pool (June–Sept daily 11am–8.30pm; €4.45), tennis courts and rowing boats for rent on the lake, all near Metro Lago. The park is best avoided after dark as many of its roads are frequented by prostitutes.

ZOO-AQUARIUM

Casa de Campo ⓜBatan ⓦzoomadrid.
com. Daily 10.30am–dusk. €22.90 (€19.90
via website). 3–7 year olds €18.55 (€16.10
via website), under-3s free. MAP P.100, POCKET
MAP A4

Laid out in sections corresponding to the five continents, Madrid's zoo, on the southwestern edge of Casa de Campo, provides decent enclosures and plenty of space for over 2000 different species. When you've had your fill of big cats, koalas and venomous snakes, you can check out the aquarium, dolphinarium, children's zoo or bird show. Boats can be rented and there are mini train tours too.

PARQUE DE ATRACCIONES

Casa de Campo ⓜBatan ⓦparquede
atracciones.es. April–Sept most days
noon–8/9pm (midnight on Sat); Oct–March
weekends and hols noon–7pm. €29.90,
children between 90–120cm €23.90, children
under 90cm free. MAP P.100, POCKET MAP A4

This is Madrid's most popular **theme park**, where highlights for adults and teenagers include the 100km/hr Abismo rollercoaster, the swirling Tarantula ride, the 63-metre vertical drop La Lanzadera, the stomach-churning La Máquina and the whitewater raft ride Los Rápidos. El Viejo Caserón is a pretty terrifying haunted house, but there are some more sedate attractions too, as well as an area for younger children. Spanish acts perform in the open-air auditorium in the summer and there are frequent parades too, plus plenty of burger/pizza places to replace lost stomach contents.

HIPÓDROMO DE LA ZARZUELA

Carretera La Coruña km 8 ⓦwww.hipodromo
delazarzuela.es. €9 for a general entry,
under-14s free. There is a free bus that
goes from Paseo de Moret next to the
Intercambiador in Moncloa. MAP P.100, POCKET
MAP A4

The **horseracing** track just out of the city on the A Coruña road is flourishing once again after a decade of neglect, and holds races every Sunday in the spring and autumn. The unstuffy atmosphere and a beautiful setting make this a fun day out for all the family.

EL PARDO

C/Manuel Alonso ⓦwww.patrimonionacional
.es. Daily: April–Sept 10am–8pm; Oct–March
10am–6pm; closed for official visits. Guided
tours €9, 5–16 year-olds €4, free for EU
citizens Wed & Thurs: April–Sept 5–8pm;

MADRID ZOO

PARQUE DE ATRACCIONES

Oct–March 3–6pm. Buses (#601) from Moncloa (daily 6.30am–midnight; every 10–15min; 25min). MAP P.100, POCKET MAP A4

Nine kilometres northwest of central Madrid lies Franco's former principal residence at El Pardo. A garrison still remains at the town, where most of the Generalíssimo's staff were based, but the place is now a popular excursion for Madrileños, who come here for long lunches at the excellent *terraza* restaurants. The tourist focus is the **Palacio del Pardo**, rebuilt by the Bourbons on the site of the hunting lodge of Carlos I and still used by visiting heads of state. Behind the imposing but blandly symmetrical facade, the interior houses the chapel where Franco prayed, and the theatre where he used to censor films. On display are a number of mementos of the dictator, including his desk, a portrait of Isabel la Católica and an excellent collection of tapestries. With its highly ornate interior, the country house retreat known as the Casita del Príncipe, designed by Prado architect Juan de Villanueva for Carlos IV and his wife María Luisa de Parma, is also open for visits after a lengthy refurbishment.

Shops

EL CORTE INGLÉS

C/Princesa 41 & 56 ⓜ Argüelles. Mon–Sat 10am–10pm. MAP P.100, POCKET MAP B1

One of many branches of Spain's biggest and most popular department store. It stocks everything from souvenirs and gift items to clothes and electrical goods. Prices are on the high side, but quality is usually very good.

OCHO Y MEDIO

C/Martín de los Heros 11 ⓜ Plaza de España ⓦ www.ochoymedio.com. Mon–Sat 10am–2pm & 5–8.30pm. MAP P.100, POCKET MAP C3

Fascinating cinema bookshop with a pleasantly anarchic collection of books and film star-backed products, as well as a great terrace and small café. Perfect for a stop before watching one of the original version films in the nearby Cines Princesa.

SANTMERY

C/Juan Álvarez Mendizábal 27 ⓜ Ventura Rodríguez. Mon–Fri 9.30am–3pm & 5.30–10pm, Sat 9.30am–3pm. MAP P.100, POCKET MAP B2

Wine shop that doubles as a bar and delicatessen. You can sample some wines by the glass and try their house speciality *mousse de cabrales a la sidra* (blue cheese and cider paté).

Café

CAFÉ MODERNO

Plaza de las Comendadoras 1 ⓜ Noviciado. Daily 1pm–2.30am. MAP P.100, POCKET MAP D2

Relaxing café-bar serving good-value drinks and snacks with a busy summer *terraza*, situated on one of the city's nicest squares. There are two other decent café-bars along-side if this one is too crowded.

Restaurants

CAFÉ DEL ORIENTE

Avda. Juan de Herrera 2 ⓜ Ciudad Universitaria ☎ 915 502 055. Tues–Sat 1.30–4.30pm & 9pm–1am. MAP P.100, POCKET MAP B1

Situated in the delightful pine-fringed grounds of the Museo del Traje, this Basque-influenced restaurant run by chef Roberto Hierro serves a seasonal menu of meat and fish dishes such as hake with Galician cockles or suckling pig with ginger, apple and fennel salad at around €22 for mains. A more economical bistro does a €16.50 lunchtime menu.

CASA MINGO

Paseo de la Florida 34 ⓜ Príncipe Pío ☎ 915 477 918. Daily 11am–midnight. Closed Aug. MAP P.100, POCKET MAP A4

Crowded and reasonably priced Asturian chicken-and-cider house. The spit-roast chicken is practically compulsory, though the *chorizo* cooked in cider and *cabrales* (blue cheese) is also very good. Around €15 a head.

LA TABERNA DE LIRIA

C/Duque de Liria 9 ⓜ Ventura Rodríguez or Plaza de España ☎ 915 414 519. Mon–Fri 1.30–3.30pm & 9.30–11.30pm, Sat 9.15–11.30pm. Closed Aug. MAP P.100, POCKET MAP C2

Excellent, low-key restaurant close to Plaza de España serving Mediterranean-style dishes with a French touch.

CASA MINGO

8

Great fish, inventive salads and delicious desserts. They provide some menu options from between €25 and €35 per head.

TOMA

C/Conde Duque 14 Ⓜ Ventura Rodríguez or Plaza de España ☎ 915 474 996. Thurs & Fri 2–4pm & 9pm–2am, Sat noon–4.30pm & 9pm–2am, Sun & hols noon–4.30pm. MAP P.100, POCKET MAP C2

Intimate restaurant with just a handful of tables in a bright red room, where husband-and-wife team Paul and Angela serve up a constantly changing menu with a creative twist. Booking is essential and budget on around €30 a head.

UROGALLO

Lago de la Casa del Campo Ⓜ Lago ☎ 915 262 369. Tues–Sun 8.30am–midnight. MAP P.100, POCKET MAP A4

On the shores of the artificial lake in Casa de Campo, this bar-restaurant has superb views of the Palacio Real and cathedral – perfect for a lazy lunch. Eating à la carte is pricey but there's a €15 lunchtime menu.

LA VACA ARGENTINA

Paseo del Pintor Rosales 52 Ⓜ Argüelles ☎ 915 596 605. Daily 1–5pm & 9pm–midnight. MAP P.100, POCKET MAP A1

One of a chain of restaurants serving Argentine-style grilled steaks (*churrasco*). This branch has good views of the Parque del Oeste from its summer terrace, but service can be slow. Average cost is around €30.

Tapas bar

CASA PACO

C/Altamirano 28 Ⓜ Argüelles ☎ 915 445 047. Mon–Sat 9am–11.30pm. MAP P.100, POCKET MAP A1

Old-style bar close to Parque del Oeste that's been around since the mid-fifties and serves

EL JARDÍN SECRETO

up some of the best tortillas in town, including tasty variations with prawns, goats cheese, spinach, and steak.

Bar

EL JARDÍN SECRETO

C/Conde Duque 2 Ⓜ Ventura Rodríguez or Plaza de España. Mon & Tues 5.30pm–12.30am, Thurs 6.30pm–1.30am, Fri & Sat 6.30pm–2.30am, Sun 5.30pm–12.30am. MAP P.100, POCKET MAP C2

Cosy, dimly lit bar on the corner of a tiny plaza close to Plaza de España serving reasonably priced drinks and cocktails. Service is friendly and the atmosphere unhurried.

Club

GALILEO GALILEI

C/Galileo 100 Ⓜ Islas Filipinas Ⓦ www.salagalileogalilei.com. Daily 6pm–4.30am. €5–10. MAP P.100, POCKET MAP C1

Bar, concert venue and disco rolled into one. Latin music is regularly on offer, along with cabaret and flamenco.

Day-trips

If you want to take a break from the frenetic activity of the city centre, there are some fascinating day-trips all within easy reach of the Spanish capital.

If you only have time for one day-trip, make it **Toledo**. The city preceded Madrid as the Spanish capital and is today a monument to the many cultures – Visigothic, Moorish, Jewish and Christian – which have shaped the destiny of Spain. Immortalized by El Greco, who lived and worked here for most of his later career, the city is packed with memorable sights. A close second is stunning **Segovia**, with its stunning Roman aqueduct, fantasy castle and mountain backdrop. Third on the list is **El Escorial**, home to Felipe II's vast monastery-palace complex, a monument to out-monument all others, although the adjacent Valle de los Caídos, built under the orders of Franco, is even more megalomaniacal and far more chilling. And not forgetting **Aranjuez**, an oasis in the parched Castilian plain famed for its strawberries, lavish Baroque palace and gardens, and the plaza at nearby **Chinchón**, which provides a fabulous setting for a long, lazy lunch.

SEGOVIA

Day-trips

N

Segovia
San Ildefonso
la Granja
Rascafría
Puerto de
los Cotos
Puerto de
Navacerrada
SIERRA DE GUADARRAMA
Manzanares
el Real
Manzanares
Jarama
A1
Valle de
los Caídos
El Escorial
A6
El Pardo
M40
R2
Alcalá de
Henares
A2
MADRID
M50
A3
R3
Getafe
M50
A5
R5
Guadarrama
AP41
A42
R4
A4
San Martín
de la Vega
Chinchón
Tajo
Aranjuez
N400
R4
Toledo

Coverage of Pocket
Madrid sheet map

0   kilometres   20
0   miles   10

Toledo

EL ALCÁZAR AND MUSEO DEL EJÉRCITO

C/Unión s/n Ⓜ www.museo.ejercito.es. Thurs–Tues 11am–5pm. €5, under-18 free, free Sun.

If one building dominates Toledo, it's the imposing fortress of the **Alcázar.** Originally the site of a Roman palace, Emperor Charles V ordered the construction of the current fortress in the sixteenth century, though it has been burned and bombarded so often that little remains of the original building. The monument enjoyed iconic status during the Franco era after the Nationalist forces inside, under siege by the Republican town, were eventually relieved by an army heading for Madrid which took severe retribution on the local inhabitants. After a tortuous relocation and refurbishment programme, the Alcázar is now home to an impressive new army museum. Encom-

passing a new building constructed over the archeological remains of the original fortress, the museum provides two fascinating routes – one historic and one thematic – through which the role of the Spanish military is examined in exhaustive detail. Exhibits include everything from medieval swords and suits of armour to toy soldiers and Civil War uniforms.

HOSPITAL Y MUSEO DE SANTA CRUZ

C/Cervantes 3. Mon–Sat 10am–6.30pm, Sun 10am–2pm. Free.

A superlative Renaissance building with a magnificent Plateresque main doorway, this newly refurbished museum houses some of the greatest El Grecos in Toledo, including *The Immaculate Conception* and *The Holy Family*. As well as outstanding works by Luca Giordano and Ribera, there's an impressive collection of exhibits dating from prehistory through to the twentieth century, including archeological finds, ceramics and sculpture.

TOLEDO

Visiting Toledo

There are **buses** to Toledo from the bus station in Plaza Elíptica (Ⓜ Plaza Elíptica) in Madrid every thirty minutes, taking about 1hr. The city's bus station is in the modern part of the city; bus #5 runs from it to central Plaza de Zocódover. A high-speed train service from Atocha takes just 30min; it's €20 for a day return ticket, but purchase this in advance (from most travel agents around the city). Toledo's train station is a 20min walk or a bus ride (#5 or #6) from the heart of town. The main **tourist office** (daily 10am–6pm; ☎ 925 254 030, ⓦ www.toledo-turismo.com) is opposite the cathedral in the Plaza del Consistorio. There's another office (Mon–Fri 10am–5pm, Sat & Sun 10am–3.50pm) at the top of the escalators leading into the city from the Glorieta de La Reconquista, and one outside the city walls opposite the Puerta Nueva de Bisagra (summer Mon–Sat 9am–7pm; winter Mon–Fri 9am–6pm, Sun & hols 9am–3pm). You can save on the entry fees to some of the sights if you invest in the €8 Bono Turístico ticket.

LA CATEDRAL

C/Cardenal Cisneros. Mon–Sat 10.30am–6.30pm, Sun 2–6.30pm. Coro closed Sun am; museums closed Mon. €7, free Sun pm for Spanish citizens; audio-guides €3.

Toledo's stunning cathedral reflects the importance of the city that for so long outshone its neighbour, Madrid. A robust Gothic construction, which took over 250 years (1227–1493) to complete, it's richly decorated in Gothic, Renaissance and Baroque styles. The cavernous interior is home to some magnificent stained glass, an outstanding **Coro** (Choir), a wonderful **Gothic Capilla Mayor** (Main Chapel) and an extravagant high altar. The cathedral **museums** are worth a look for their impressive collections including paintings by El Greco, Goya and Velázquez, as well as one of El Greco's few surviving pieces of sculpture.

SANTO TOMÉ AND THE BURIAL OF THE COUNT OF ORGAZ

Plaza del Conde ⓦ www.santotome.org. Daily: mid-March–mid-Oct 10am–6.45pm; mid-Oct–mid-March 10am–5.45pm. €2.30.

Housed alone, in a small annexe of the church of Santo Tomé, one of the most celebrated attractions of Toledo is El Greco's masterpiece, *The Burial of the Count of Orgaz*. The painting depicts the count's funeral, at which St Stephen and St Augustine appeared in order to lower him into the tomb. Combining El Greco's genius for the mystic with his great powers as a portrait painter and master of colour, the work includes a depiction of the artist himself – he can be spotted seventh from the left, looking out at the viewer with his son in the foreground.

MUSEO DEL GRECO

C/Samuel Levi ⓦ museodelgreco.mcu.es. April–Sept Tues–Sat 9.30am–8.30pm, Sun 10am–3pm; May–Oct Tues–Sat 9.30am–6.30pm, Sun 10am–3pm. €3, €5 entry with Museo Sefardí, free Sat 4–6.30pm & Sun.

This museum in the former Jewish quarter close to Santo Tomé is devoted to the life and work of the ground-breaking sixteenth-century artist so closely associated with Toledo. A refurbished exhibition space houses his famous **View and Map of Toledo**, a series of the Twelve Apostles, completed later than the set in the cathedral, and other outstanding works.

There are plenty of bars and restaurants scattered around the old town, although inevitably most of the options are pretty touristy. For a budget option try *Casa Ludeña* at Plaza Magdalena 13, close to the Alcázar, while *Casa Aurelio* at C/Sinagoga 1 & 6, near the cathedral, offers regional specialities at reasonable prices. For a more sophisticated option try *Los Cuatro Tiempos* at C/Sixto Ramón Parro 5.

MUSEO DE VICTORIO MACHO

Plaza de Victorio Macho ⓦwww
.realfundaciontoledo.es. Mon–Sat 10am–7pm,
Sun 10am–3pm. €3.

Splendidly situated on a spur overlooking the Tajo, this museum contains the sculptures, paintings and sketches of Spanish artist Victorio Macho (1887–1966). The museum is set in a delightfully tranquil garden with the auditorium on the ground floor showing a documentary film (available in English) about the city and its history.

MUSEO SEFARDÍ/SINAGOGA DEL TRÁNSITO

C/Samuel Levi ⓦmuseosefardi.mcu.es. Tues–
Sat 9.30am–6pm (summer till 8pm),
Sun 10am–3pm. €3, free Sat after 2pm
& Sun.

Built along Moorish lines by Samuel Levi in 1366, the Sinagoga del Tránsito became a church after the fifteenth-century expulsion of the Jews and was restored to its original form only in the last century. The interior is a simple galleried hall, brilliantly decorated with polychromed stuccowork and superb filigree windows, while Hebrew inscriptions praising God, King Pedro and Samuel Levi adorn the walls. It also houses a small but engaging Sephardic Museum (same hours) tracing the distinct traditions and development of Jewish culture in Spain.

SINAGOGA SANTA MARÍA LA BLANCA

C/Reyes Católicos 4. Daily: summer
10am–6.45pm; winter 10am–5.45pm. €2.50,
free Wed after 4pm for EU citizens.

The second of Toledo's two surviving synagogues, the tranquil Santa María la Blanca pre-dates the Sinagoga del Tránsito by over a century. Despite having been both a church and synagogue, the horseshoe arches and the fact that it was built by Mudéjar craftsmen give it the look of a mosque. The arches are decorated with elaborate plaster designs of pine cones and palm trees, while its Baroque *retablo* (altarpiece) dates from the time it was a church. The whole effect is stunning, all set off against a deep-red floor that contains some of the original decorative tiles.

MONASTERIO DE SAN JUAN DE LOS REYES

C/San Juan de los Reyes 2. Daily: summer
10am–6.30pm; winter 10am–5.30pm. €2.50.

The exterior of this beautiful church is bizarrely festooned with the chains worn by Christian prisoners from Granada, who were released on the reconquest of the city in 1492. It was originally a **Franciscan convent** founded by the Reyes Católicos (Catholic Monarchs) Fernando and Isabel – who completed the Christian reconquest of Spain – and in which, until the fall of Granada, they had planned to be buried. Its double-storeyed cloister is outstanding, with an elaborate Mudéjar ceiling in the upper floor.

CONVENTO DE SANTO DOMINGO ANTIGUO

Plaza Santo Domingo Antiguo. Summer: Mon–Sat 11am–1.30pm & 4–7pm, Sun 4–7pm. €2.

The Convento de Santo Domingo Antiguo's chief claim to fame is as the resting place of El Greco, whose remains lie in the crypt that can be glimpsed through a peephole in the floor. The convent's religious treasures are displayed in the old choir, but more interesting is the high altarpiece of the church – El Greco's first major commission in Toledo. Unfortunately, most of the canvases have gone to museums and are here replaced by copies.

MEZQUITA DEL CRISTO DE LA LUZ

Cuesta de los Carmelitas Descalzos 10. Summer: Mon–Fri 10am–2pm & 3.30–6.40pm, Sat & Sun: 10am–6.40pm; winter: Mon–Fri 10am–2pm & 3.30–5.45pm, Sat & Sun 10am–5.45pm. €2.50.

Although this is one of the oldest Moorish monuments in Spain (the mosque was built by Musa Ibn Ali in the tenth century on the foundations of a Visigothic church), only the nave, with its nine different cupolas, is the original Arab construction. The apse was added when the building was converted into a church, and is claimed to be the first product of the Mudéjar style. The mosque itself, set in a tiny patio-like park and open on all sides to the elements, is so small that it seems more like a miniature summer pavilion, but it has an elegant simplicity of design that few of the town's great monuments can match.

CATHEDRAL, TOLEDO

Segovia

THE AQUEDUCT

Plaza del Azoguejo.

Over 700m long and almost 30m high, Segovia's aqueduct is an impressive sight. Built without a drop of mortar or cement, it has been here since around the end of the first century AD – no one knows exactly when – though it no longer carries water to the city. For an excellent view of both the aqueduct and the city, climb the stairs beside it up to a surviving fragment of the city walls.

THE CATHEDRAL

Plaza Mayor. Daily: April–Sept 9.30am–6.30pm; Oct–March 9.30am–5.30pm. €3. Museum: Sun 9.30am–1.15pm.

Segovia's cathedral was the last major Gothic building constructed in Spain. Pinnacles and flying buttresses are tacked on at every conceivable point, although the interior is surprisingly bare and its space is cramped by a great green marble choir in the very centre. The cathedral's treasures are almost all confined to the museum.

THE ALCÁZAR

Plaza Reina Victoria Eugenia ⓦ www .alcazardesegovia.com. Daily: April–Sept 10am–7pm; Oct–March 10am–6pm. €4.50, free for EU citizens third Tues in the month.

At the edge of town and overlooking the valley of the Eresma river is the Alcázar, an extraordinary fantasy of a castle with its narrow towers and flurry of turrets. Although it dates from the fourteenth and fifteenth centuries, it was almost completely destroyed by a fire in 1862 and rebuilt as a deliberately exaggerated version of the original. Inside, the rooms are decked out with armour, weapons and tapestries, but the major attractions are the splendid wooden sculptured ceilings and the magnificent panoramas.

VERA CRUZ

Carretera Zamarramala. Summer Tues 4–7pm, Wed–Sun 10.30am–1.30pm & 4–7pm; winter Tues–Sun 10.30am–1.30pm & 4–7pm. Closed Nov. €2, free Tues.

This remarkable twelve-sided church stands in the valley facing the Alcázar. Built by the Knights Templar in the early thirteenth century on the pattern of the Church of the Holy Sepulchre in Jerusalem,

Visiting Segovia

Segovia is an easy day-trip from Madrid, with up to ten high-speed trains daily (28min; €25 return) from Atocha and Chamartín stations, plus **buses** operated by La Sepulvedana leaving from Paseo de la Florida 11 (Metro Príncipe Pío; every 30min; 1hr 45min). The high-speed train station is out of town – take bus #11 (every 15min) to the aqueduct. There's a local **tourist office** in the Plaza Mayor at no. 9 (Mon–Fri 8am–3pm; ⓦsegoviaturismo.es) and a regional one at no. 10 (Mon–Sat 10am–2pm & 4–7/8pm, Sun 9.30am–5pm; ⓦturismocastillayleon.com). A visitor reception centre is situated in the Plaza de Azoguejo (daily 10am–7pm) by the aqueduct and an information point at the high-speed train station (Mon–Fri 8.15am–3.15pm, Sat & Sun 10am–2.15pm & 4–5.45pm). A regular bus service from Segovia to La Granja is operated by La Sepulvedana, leaving from the station at Paseo Ezequiel González 12.

THE AQUEDUCT, SEGOVIA

it once housed part of the supposed True Cross (hence its name). Today, you can climb the tower for a highly photogenic view of the city, while nearby is a very pleasant riverside walk along the banks of the tranquil Eresma river.

CONVENTO DE SAN ANTONIO REAL

C/San Antonio Real. Tues–Sat 10am–2pm & 4–6.30pm, Sun 10.30am–2pm. €2.

If you follow the line of the aqueduct away from the old city for about ten minutes, you will come to a little gem of a palace originally founded by Enrique IV in 1455 and containing an intriguing collection of Mudéjar and Hispano-Flemish art. The convent has some of the most beautiful **artesonado** (wooden sculptured) ceilings in the city and there's a wonderfully detailed fifteenth-century wooden Calvary in the main church.

LA GRANJA

ⓦ www.patrimonionacional.es. Palace open daily: April–Sept 10am–8pm; Oct–March 10am–6pm. €9; free Wed & Thurs: April–Sept 5–8pm; Oct–March 3–6pm. Gardens daily: 10am–dusk.

The summer palace of La Granja was built by the first Bourbon king of Spain, Felipe V, no doubt in another attempt to alleviate his homesickness for Versailles. Its chief appeal lies in its mountain setting and extravagant wooded grounds and gardens, but it's also worth casting an eye over the plush furnishings and fabulous tapestries of the palace which, though damaged by a fire in 1918, has been successfully restored.

Outside, the highlight of the eighteenth-century gardens is a series of majestic fountains. They're a fantastic spectacle, with some of the jets rising forty metres, but they usually only operate at 5.30pm at weekends and on Wednesdays between Easter and July, with special displays on May 30, July 25 and August 25 (€4).

🍴 Segovia is renowned for its delicious Castilian roasts; some of the best places to sample the local specialities are the *Mesón José María* at c/Cronista Lecea 11, just off the Plaza Mayor, *Mesón de Cándido* below the aqueduct at Plaza Azoguejo 5 and *Casa Duque* at nearby C/Cervantes 12.

El Escorial and Valle de los Caídos

EL ESCORIAL

W www.patrimonionacional.es. Tues–Sun: April–Sept 10am–8pm; Oct–March 10am–6pm. €10 guided; free Wed & Thurs: April–Sept 5–8pm; Oct–March 3–6pm.

El Escorial was the largest Spanish building of the Renaissance, built to celebrate a victory over the French in 1557 and divided into different sections for secular and religious use. Linking the two zones is the Biblioteca (Library), a splendid hall with vivid, multicoloured frescoes by Tibaldi, and containing some gorgeously executed Arabic manuscripts.

The enormous, cold, dark interior of the Basílica contains over forty altars, designed to allow simultaneous Masses to be held. Behind the main altar lies some of Felipe II's mammoth collection of saintly relics, including six whole bodies, over sixty heads and hundreds of bone fragments set in fabulously expensive caskets.

Many of the monastery's religious treasures are contained in the Sacristía and Salas Capitulares and include paintings by Titian, Velázquez and José Ribera. Below these rooms is the Panteón Real, where past Spanish monarchs lie in their gilded marble tombs. The royal children are laid in the Panteón de los Infantes and there's also a babies' tomb with room for sixty infants.

What remains of El Escorial's art collection – works by Bosch, Dürer, Titian, Zurbarán, among others that escaped transfer to the Prado – is kept in the elegant Museos Nuevos. Don't miss the Sala de Batallas, a long gallery lined with an epic series of paintings depicting important imperial battles. Finally, there are the treasure-crammed Salones

EL ESCORIAL

Reales (Royal Apartments), containing the austere quarters of Felipe II, with the chair that supported his gouty leg and the deathbed from which he was able to contemplate the high altar of the Basílica.

LA SILLA DE FELIPE

Around 3km out of town is the Silla de Felipe – "Felipe's Seat" – a chair carved into a rocky outcrop with a great view of the palace, and from where the king is supposed to have watched the building's construction. You can reach it on foot by following the path which starts by the arches beyond the main entrance to the Biblioteca; keep to the left as you go down the hill and then cross the main road and follow the signs. If you have a car, take the M-505 Ávila road and turn off at the sign after about 3km.

VALLE DE LOS CAÍDOS

Tues–Sun: April–Sept 10am–7pm; Oct–March 10am–6pm. €9; free Wed & Thurs pm for EU citizens.

Almost at first glance, this basilica complex, constructed by Franco after his Civil War victory, belies its claim to be a memorial to the dead of both sides. The grim, pompous architectural forms employed, the constant inscriptions "Fallen for God and for

(icon) Good restaurants in El Escorial include *La Fonda Genara* at Plaza de San Lorenzo 2 (daily 1–4pm & 9–11.30pm; ☎ 918 901 636), a relaxed place filled with theatrical mementos and offering a wide range of delicious Castilian cuisine. *Menús* available for around €15, otherwise around €30 per person.

Spain" and the proximity to El Escorial clue you in to its true function – the glorification of General Franco and his regime. The dictator himself lies buried behind the high altar, while the only other named tomb is that of his guru, the Falangist leader, José Antonio Primo de Rivera. The "other side" is present only in the fact that the whole thing was built by the Republican army's survivors.

Above the basilica is a vast 150m-high cross, reputedly the largest in the world and visible for miles around. The socialist government of José Luis Rodríguez Zapatero tried to depoliticize the site, and it was mooted that Franco's remains might be removed from the basilica, but this was rejected when the new right-of-centre Popular Party returned to power in the 2011 general election.

Visiting El Escorial

There are around 25 **trains** a day to El Escorial from Madrid (5.45am–11.30pm from Atocha, calling at Chamartín), or **buses** (#661 and #664 from the intercambiador at Moncloa) run every fifteen minutes on weekdays and hourly at weekends. To visit the Valle de los Caídos from El Escorial, take a local bus run by Herranz (#660), which starts from their office in Plaza de la Virgen de Gracia, just north of the visitors' entrance to the monastery. It runs from El Escorial at 3.15pm, returning at 5.30pm (Tues–Sun; €4.40 return).

Aranjuez and Chinchón

THE PALACIO REAL

🌐 www.patrimonionacional.es. Daily: April–Sept 10am–8pm; Oct–March 10am–6pm. €9; free for EU citizens Wed & Thurs: April–Sept 5–8pm; Oct–March 3–5pm.

The centrepiece of Aranjuez is the Palacio Real and its gardens. The present building dates from the 1700s and was an attempt by Spain's Bourbon monarchs to create a Spanish Versailles. The palace is noted for its exotic decor highlighted in the fabulously elaborate Porcelain and Smoking Rooms.

JARDÍN DE LA ISLA AND JARDÍN DEL PRÍNCIPE

Daily: 8am–dusk. Free.

Two palace gardens worthy of a visit are the Jardín de la Isla with its fountains and neatly tended gardens, and the more attractive Jardín del Príncipe, which inspired Rodrigo's famous *Concierto de Aranjuez*, offering shaded walks

🍴 *El Rana Verde* close to the palace and on the banks of the river at Plaza Santiago Rusiñol is probably Aranjuez's best-known restaurant and serves a selection of *menús* from €17.

along the river and plenty of spots for a siesta.

CASA DEL LABRADOR

Jardín del Príncipe. Daily: April–Sept 10am–8pm; Oct–March 10am–6pm; visits by appointment only ☎ 918 910 305. €9; free for EU citizens Wed & Thurs: April–Sept 5–8pm; Oct–March 3–5pm.

At the far end of the Jardín del Príncipe is the Casa del Labrador (Peasant's House), which is anything but what its name implies. The house contains more silk, marble, crystal and gold than would seem possible to cram into so small a place, as well as a huge collection of fancy clocks. Although the hotchpotch of styles will offend purists, this miniature palace still provides a fascinating insight into the

THE SMOKING ROOMS AT PALACIO REAL, ARANJUEZ

Visiting Aranjuez and Chinchón

From the end of April to July and September to mid-October, a weekend service on an old wooden steam train, the **Tren de la Fresa**, runs between Madrid and Aranjuez. It leaves the Museo del Ferrocarril at 9.50am and departs from Aranjuez at 6.30pm (information ☎ 902 228 822). The €29 fare (children aged 4–12 years €21) includes a guided bus tour in Aranjuez, entry to the monuments and *fresas con nata* on the train. Standard trains leave every 15–30min from Atocha, with the last train returning from Aranjuez at about 11.30pm. **Buses** run every half-hour during the week and every hour at weekends from Estación Sur. You'll find a helpful **tourist office** in the Casa de Infantes (daily 9.30am–6pm; ☎ 918 910 427, ⬤ www .aranjuez.es). There are hourly buses (#337) from Madrid **to Chinchón** from the bus station at Avda Mediterraneo 49 near the Plaza Conde Casal, or you can reach the town from Aranjuez on the sporadic service from c/Almíbar 138 (Mon–Fri 4 daily, Sat 2 daily). There's a small **tourist office** in the Plaza Mayor (July–Sept Mon–Fri 10am–3pm & 4–8pm, Sat & Sun 10am–3pm; Oct–June daily 10am–7pm ☎ 918 935 323, ⬤ ciudad-chinchon.com).

tastes of the Bourbon dynasty.

CASA DE LOS MARINOS (FALÚAS REALES)

Daily: April–Sept 10am–8pm; Oct–March 10am–6pm. €9; free for EU citizens Wed & Thurs: April–Sept 5–8pm; Oct–March 3–5pm.
The small Casa de los Marinos museum contains the brightly coloured launches in which royalty would take to the river – try the modern equivalent with a 45-minute boat trip through the royal parks from the jetty by the bridge next to the palace (summer: Tues–Sun 11am– sunset; €7, under-13s €4).

PLAZA DE TOROS

Guided tours: Mon 11.15am, 12.15pm, 1.15pm, Sat & Sun 11.15am, 12.15pm, 1.15pm, 4.15pm; €5.
Aranjuez's beautiful eighteenth-century Plaza de Toros houses an exhibition space, part of which is made up of a **bullfighting museum**, while the rest traces the town's history and royal heritage. Nearby, on C/Naranja and C/Rosa, there are a number of *corrales*, traditional-style wooden-balconied tenement blocks.

CHINCHÓN

A stroll around the elegant little town of Chinchón, followed by lunch at one of its restaurants, is a popular pastime for Madrileños. Noteworthy monuments include a fifteenth-century castle (not open to visitors), a picture-postcard medieval Plaza Mayor and the Iglesia de la Asunción, with a panel by Goya of *The Assumption of the Virgin*, but it is as the home of *anís* that the town is best known. To sample the local aniseed spirit try one of the local bars or the Alcoholera de Chinchón, a shop on the Plaza Mayor – most visitors come for a tasting before eating at one of the town's traditional *mesones* (see box below).

For a classic Castillian lunch in Chinchón try the *Mesón el Comendador*, *La Casa del Pregonero* or *La Balconada* overlooking the main plaza or the nearby *Mesón Cuevas del Vino*.

Accommodation

Madrid has a plentiful supply of accommodation and most of it is very central. With increasing competition in the sector, many hotels have been busy upgrading facilities in recent years and there is now a much wider range of stylish, medium-priced hotels, including the design-conscious High Tech and Room Mate chains. The city has a sprinkling of exclusive top-range hotels too, while if you're after a budget place to stay go for one of the *hostales* – small, frequently family-run establishments housed in large, centrally located apartment blocks.

The main factor to consider in choosing a place is location. To be at the heart of the old town, choose the areas around Puerta del Sol, Plaza de Santa Ana or Plaza Mayor; for nightlife, Malasaña or Chueca will appeal; if you are looking for a quieter location and a bit more luxury, consider the Paseo del Prado, Recoletos or Salamanca areas; and if you are with children the areas by the main parks are good options. Another thing to bear in mind is noise. Madrid is a high-decibel city so avoid rooms on lower floors or choose a place away from the action. As for facilities, air conditioning is usual and a welcome extra in summer.

Prices given in our reviews are for the cheapest double room available.

Booking accommodation

Madrid's increasing popularity as a weekend-break destination means that it's best to book accommodation in advance. Phoning or emailing is recommended; most places will understand English. It's also advisable to reconfirm the booking a few days in advance.

Hotels in the more expensive categories run special weekend offers, so it's always worth checking their websites for details. Many travel agents have voucher schemes which are a great way of making huge savings on standard rates – they're available at travel agents and online at sites such as ⓦ www.bancotel.com.

If you do arrive without a reservation, accommodation services at the airport, the Estación Sur de Autobuses, and Atocha and Chamartín train stations can be a useful fallback.

Madrid de los Austrias

BED & BREAKFAST ABRACADABRA
> C/Bailén 39, 1° Ⓜ Ópera or La Latina
☎ 656 859 784, Ⓦ www.abracadabra
bandb.com. MAP P.30–31, POCKET
MAP C7. A homely seven-bedroom
B&B run by a very friendly couple who
have refurbished the place in rustic,
colonial style. Some rooms have en-suite
bathrooms. Continental breakfast
included in the rate. Doubles with shared
bathroom from €54. **En-suite doubles
from €71.**

CHIC & BASIC MAYERLING >
C/Conde de Romanones 6 Ⓜ Tirso de
Molina ☎ 914 201 580, Ⓦ www
.chicandbasic.com. MAP P.30–31,
POCKET MAP D13. A stylish hotel with
22 rooms, housed in a former textile
warehouse close to C/Atocha. Clean lines
and black and white decor predominate
in the simple, neat rooms. Continental
breakfast is included and there's free
internet and wi-fi as well as a sun
terrace. **Doubles from €80.**

HOSTAL LA MACARENA > C/Cava de
San Miguel 8, 2° Ⓜ Sol ☎ 913 659 221,
Ⓦ www.silserranos.com. MAP P.30–31,
POCKET MAP B13. Family-run *hostal* in a
back street just beside Plaza Mayor. The
neat, well-kept rooms are on the small
side, but all have bathroom, satellite TV
and a/c. It can be a little noisy, but the
location is perfect. **Doubles from €59.**

HOSTAL TIJCAL > C/Zaragoza 6, 3°
Ⓜ Sol ☎ 913 655 910, Ⓦ www
.hostaltijcal.com. MAP P.30–31, POCKET
MAP C12. Quirky *hostal* offering rooms
(some have good views) in pastel shades
with bathroom, TV, very comfortable beds
and a/c. Triples and quadruples also
available. A sister *hostal*, Tijcal II, is at
C/Cruz 26 (☎ 913 604 628). **Doubles
from €40.**

HOTEL PLAZA MAYOR > C/Atocha 2
Ⓜ Sol ☎ 913 600 606, Ⓦ www
.h-plazamayor.com. MAP P.30–31,
POCKET MAP D13. A stone's throw
from the Plaza Mayor and housed in
a refurbished historic building, this
good-value and friendly hotel has 33

bright, a/c rooms. **Doubles from €60.**

PETIT PALACE POSADA DEL PEINE
> C/Postas 17 Ⓜ Sol ☎ 915 238 151,
Ⓦ www.hthotels.com. MAP P.30–31,
POCKET MAP C12. This upmarket branch
of the *High Tech* hotel chain is situated
in a refurbished building right next to the
Plaza Mayor and was once the site of a
seventeenth-century inn. Sleek rooms
with minimalist decor and stylish fittings.
Buffet breakfast. **Doubles from €100.**

POSADA DEL LEÓN DE ORO >
C/Cava Baja 12 Ⓜ La Latina ☎ 911
191 494, Ⓦ www.posadadelleondeoro.
com. MAP P. 30–31, POCKET MAP B14.
This former inn has been converted into a
chic, designer hotel with seventeen large,
individually decorated rooms complete
with walk-in showers, flat-screen TVs and
free wi-fi. **Doubles from €100.**

Ópera

LOS AMIGOS HOSTEL > C/Arenal 26,
4° Ⓜ Ópera ☎ 915 592 472, Ⓦ www
.losamigoshostel.com. MAP P.40,
POCKET MAP B11. Great backpacking
option just a few minutes from Sol.
Dormitories (€17–19 per bed) cater for
4–6 people, and there are a couple of
communal rooms, plus free wi-fi. The
staff speak English, and bed linen and
use of kitchen are included. **Doubles
with bathroom from €50.**

CASA MADRID > C/Arrieta 2, 2°
Ⓜ Ópera ☎ 660 342 427, Ⓦ www
.casademadrid.com. MAP P.40, POCKET
MAP B10. Exclusive boutique hotel, with
seven stunning rooms decorated with
hand-painted frescoes, classical statues
and fresh flowers. Ideal for an expensive
romantic escape, but not really the place
for children. **Doubles from €140.**

HOSTAL DON ALFONSO > Plaza
Celenque 1, 2° Ⓜ Sol ☎ 915 319 840
Ⓦ www.hostaldonalfonso.es. MAP P.40,
POCKET MAP C11. Just off the
pedestrianized shopping street C/Arenal and
a stone's throw from Sol, this clean, simply
furnished *hostal* has 14 doubles, two triples
and some singles, all with bathrooms, a/c
and TV. **Doubles from €50.**

HOSTAL GALA > C/Costanilla de los Ángeles 15 Ⓜ Callao ☎ 915 419 692, Ⓦ www.hostalgala.com. MAP P.40, POCKET MAP B10. An upmarket, very tasteful *hostal* close to the shopping areas of C/Preciados and Gran Vía. The 22 rooms have a/c, power showers and small balconies. **Doubles from €60.**

HOSTAL ORIENTE > C/Arenal 23 Ⓜ Ópera ☎ 915 480 314, Ⓦ www.hostaloriente.es. MAP P.40, POCKET MAP B11. Well-appointed *hostal* close to the Opera house. The nineteen classically decorated rooms are comfortable and have newly equipped bathrooms. **Doubles from €55.**

HOTEL CARLOS V > C/Maestro Vitoria 5 Ⓜ Callao ☎ 915 314 100, Ⓦ www.hotelcarlosv-madrid.com. MAP P.40, POCKET MAP D11. Traditional hotel behind the Descalzas Reales monastery. Some of the a/c rooms on the fifth floor have balconies (at extra cost), though there isn't much of a view. There's an elegant lounge and café, and the hotel has a deal with a nearby car park allowing guests to use it at reduced rates. **Doubles from €75.**

HOTEL MENINAS > C/Campomanes 7 Ⓜ Ópera ☎ 915 412 805, Ⓦ www.hotelmeninas.com. MAP P.40, POCKET MAP B10. A stylish 37-room hotel in a quiet street near the Teatro Real. Professional staff, fantastic attic rooms and flat-screen TVs. Guests can use the gym and sauna at the nearby *Hotel Ópera* (see below). Breakfast included for web reservations. Prices vary according to availability but usually **doubles from €95.**

HOTEL ÓPERA > C/Cuesta de Santo Domingo 2 Ⓜ Ópera ☎ 915 412 800, Ⓦ www.hotelopera.com. MAP P.40, POCKET MAP B10. In a pleasant location near the Plaza de Oriente, this slick hotel has 79 smart rooms (some with terraces) at reasonable rates. In keeping with the name, the waiters in the restaurant entertain diners with arias from operas and zarzuelas. **Doubles from €95.**

HOTEL PALACIO DE SAN MARTÍN > Plaza de San Martín 5 Ⓜ Ópera

☎ 917 015 000, Ⓦ www.hotelpalaciosanmartin.es. MAP P.40, POCKET MAP C10. Situated in an attractive square by the Descalzas Reales monastery, this elegant hotel offers 94 spacious rooms, a small gym and sauna, plus a fine rooftop restaurant. **Doubles from €105.**

PETIT PALACE ARENAL > C/Arenal 16 Ⓜ Sol ☎ 915 644 355, Ⓦ www.hthoteles.com. MAP P.40, POCKET MAP C11. A member of the *High Tech* hotel chain with 64 sleek, modern rooms. All have a/c and there are special family rooms too. Another member of the chain, the *Puerta del Sol*, is close by at C/Arenal 4. **Doubles from €90.**

POSADA REAL MANUEL > Plaza de Oriente 2, 3° Ⓜ Ópera ☎ 915 598 450, Ⓦ www.posadarealmanuel.com. MAP P.40, POCKET MAP A11. This seven-room *posada* has a fabulous location with great views over the plaza towards the Palacio Real. **Doubles from €75.**

ROOM MATE MARIO > C/Campomanes 4 Ⓜ Ópera ☎ 915 488 548, Ⓦ www.roomatehotels.com. MAP P.40, POCKET MAP B10. Hip designer hotel close to the Teatro Real. Staff are friendly and the ultra-cool rooms, though compact, are well equipped with neat bathrooms, flat-screen TVs and DVD. Buffet breakfast included in price. There is a similarly trendy member of the chain, the *Laura*, at Travesía de Trujillos 3 (☎ 917 011 670) in the plaza by the Descalzas monastery. **Doubles from €90.**

Rastro, Lavapiés and Embajadores

CAT'S HOSTEL > C/Canizares 6 Ⓜ Antón Martín ☎ 913 692 807, Ⓦ www.catshostel.com. MAP P.48–49, POCKET MAP E14. Certainly not your run-of-the-mill hostel, *Cat's* has an Andalusian patio and subterranean bar. Doubles are available on request, otherwise accommodation is in clean, a/c four–twelve-bed dorms. Price includes breakfast. **Dorm bed from €14.**

HOSTAL BARRERA ⟩ C/Atocha 96, 2°
Ⓜ Antón Martín ☎ 915 275 381,
Ⓦ www.hostalbarrera.com. MAP
P.48–49, POCKET MAP G7. Upmarket
fourteen-room *hostal* a short distance
from Atocha station and with an
English-speaking owner. The smart a/c
rooms are a cut above most found in this
category and the bathrooms are modern.
One of the best in this part of town.
Doubles from €65.

TRYP ATOCHA ⟩ C/Atocha 83
Ⓜ Antón Martín ☎ 913 300 500,
Ⓦ www.tryphotels.com.
MAP P.48–49, POCKET MAP G14. This
large, business-style hotel, which is not
far from Huertas, has 150 modern rooms
with all the facilities you'd expect. Family
rooms with bunks for children start at
€160. **Doubles from €98.**

Sol, Santa Ana and Huertas

CATALONIA PLAZA MAYOR ⟩ C/
Atocha 35 Ⓜ Antón Martín ☎ 913 694
409, Ⓦ www.hoteles-catalonia.com.
MAP P.54, POCKET MAP E13 Close to
Plaza Santa Ana and the Huertas area, this
new business-style hotel has spacious,
functional rooms with slick modern decor
and comfortable beds. There's a small
fitness area and jacuzzi as well as free
wi-fi. **Doubles from €100.**

CHIC & BASIC COLORS ⟩ C/Huertas
14, 2° izda Ⓜ Antón Martín ☎ 914
296 935, Ⓦ www.chicandbasic.com.
MAP P.54, POCKET MAP F13. Swish
hostal in the heart of Huertas with ten
design-conscious en-suite rooms, all
complete with a/c and plasma TVs. There
is a self-service breakfast and a common
room where you can read the paper.
Doubles from €60.

HOSTAL ALASKA ⟩ C/Espoz y Mina 7,
4° dcha Ⓜ Sol ☎ 915 211 845, Ⓦ www
.hostalalaska.es. MAP P.54, POCKET MAP
E12. Doubles, triples and a single in this
friendly *hostal*. All seven of the basic,
brightly decorated rooms have bathrooms,
a/c and TV. There's an apartment available

Our picks

Friendly – *Hostal Gonzalo* p.126
Good value – *Hostal Gala* p.124
Boutique – *Abalú* p.128
Designer chic – *Urban* p.126
Romantic – *Casa Madrid* p.123
Celeb-spotting – *Santo Mauro*
p.129
Family – *Tirol* p.129

on the fifth floor with a bedroom, sofa-bed
and kitchen (from €100 for six). **Doubles
from €52.**

HOSTAL ARMESTO ⟩ C/San Agustín 6,
1° dcha Ⓜ Antón Martín ☎ 914 299 031,
Ⓦ www.hostalarmesto.com. MAP P.54,
POCKET MAP G13. Eight-room *hostal* with
some nicely decorated rooms, all with
small bathrooms, a/c and TV. The best
ones overlook the delightful little garden
in the Casa de Lope de Vega next door.
Very well positioned for the Huertas/Santa
Ana area. **Doubles from €40.**

HOSTAL PERSAL ⟩ Plaza del Angel 12
Ⓜ Sol ☎ 913 694 643, Ⓦ www
.hostalpersal.com. MAP P.54, POCKET
MAP E13. Eighty-room *hostal* that's
closer to a hotel in terms of services and
facilities. The simple, clean rooms all have
a/c, bathrooms, TV and free wi-fi. Triples
and quadruples available from €90 and
€110 respectively. **Doubles from €69.**

HOSTAL PLAZA D'ORT ⟩ Plaza del
Angel 13, 1° Ⓜ Sol ☎ 914 299 041,
Ⓦ www.plazadort.com. MAP P.54,
POCKET MAP E13. All the smallish rooms
in this very clean *hostal* have a shower
or bath, TV, telephone and internet
connection, and some have a/c too.
Doubles from €55.

HOSTAL RIESCO ⟩ C/Correo 2, 3°
Ⓜ Sol ☎ 915 222 692, Ⓦ www
.hostalriesco.es. MAP P.54, POCKET
MAP D12. Neat and simple rooms in this
friendly family-run *hostal* located in a
street just off Sol. All rooms (some of
which are triples) are en suite and have
a/c. **Doubles from €55.**

ACCOMMODATION

HOTEL URBAN > Carrera San Jeronimo 34 ⓜ Sevilla ☎ 917 877 770, ⓦ www.derbyhotels.com. MAP P.54, POCKET MAP G12. Über cool, fashion-conscious, five-star hotel in the heart of town. There are 96 designer rooms with all mod cons, a rooftop pool, a summer terrace and two "pijo" cocktail bars. It even has its own small museum consisting of items from owner Jordi Clos's collection of Egyptian and Chinese art. Look out for special deals on the website. **Doubles from €175.**

HOTEL VINCCI SOHO > C/Prado 18 ⓜ Antón Martín ☎ 911 414 100, ⓦ www.vinccihoteles.com. MAP P.54, POCKET MAP G13. A great location in the heart of Huertas for this new, four-star 170-room hotel. Smart wooden decor and furnishings and modern facilities, though bathrooms are rather small. Worth it only if you can get one of the cheaper offers on the website. **Doubles from €110.**

INTERNATIONAL HOSTEL POSADA DE HUERTAS > C/Huertas 21 ⓜ Ciudad de los Ángeles ☎ 914 295 526, ⓦ www.posadadehuertas.com. MAP P.54, POCKET MAP F13. A modern hostel right at the heart of things, close to Plaza Santa Ana. A/c dormitories range in size from four to ten berths (breakfast included). There's a common room with TV and internet access, laundry facilities and individual lockers. **From €17.**

ME MADRID > Plaza de Santa Ana 14 ⓜ Sol ☎ 917 016 000, ⓦ www.memadrid.com. MAP P.54, POCKET MAP E13. Once a favourite haunt of bullfighters, this giant white wedding cake of a hotel that dominates the plaza is now part of the exclusive ME chain. It comes complete with all the de rigueur minimalist decor, designer furnishings, high-tech fittings, a super cool penthouse bar and a chic restaurant serving fusion-style food. Special offers can bring the price down to around €150, but usually **doubles from €200.**

PETIT PALACE LONDRES > C/Galdo 2 ⓜ Sol ☎ 915 314 105, ⓦ www.hthotels.com. MAP P.54, POCKET MAP D11. One of a chain of the

smart *High Tech* hotels that offer very good rates and services. This one is in a refurbished mansion close to Sol and has the trademark smart, well-appointed rooms with a range of facilities. **Doubles from €70.**

ROOM MATE ALICIA > C/Prado 2 ⓜ Sol ☎ 913 896 095, ⓦ www.room -matehotels.com. MAP P.54, POCKET MAP F13. Perched on the corner of Plaza Santa Ana, the 34-room *Alicia* is in a great location, if a little noisy. Seriously cool decor by interior designer Pascua Ortega, stylish rooms and unbeatable value. There are suites from €145 with great views over the plaza and if you really want to push the boat out there is a two-floored duplex at around €275. **Doubles from €90.**

Paseo del Arte and Retiro

CHIC & BASIC ATOCHA > C/Atocha 113, 3° ⓜ Atocha ☎ 913 692 895, ⓦ www.chicandbasic .com. MAP P.68–69, POCKET MAP G7. Just across the roundabout from Atocha station, this branch of the *Chic & Basic* chain contains 36 sleek but simple rooms at a very competitive price. A sun terrace on the sixth floor and complimentary coffee in the "help yourself" zone. **Doubles from €90.**

HOSTAL GONZALO > C/Cervantes 34, 3° ⓜ Antón Martín ☎ 914 292 714, ⓦ www.hostalgonzalo.com. MAP P.68–69, POCKET MAP H13. One of the most welcoming *hostales* in the city, tucked away close to Paseo del Prado. Fifteen bright, en-suite rooms, all of which have a/c, TV and recently refurbished bathrooms as well as free wi-fi. It's a very good-value, smart place run by charming owner Antonio and his brother Javier. **Doubles from €50.**

HOTEL LOPE DE VEGA > C/Lope de Vega 49 ⓜ Atocha ☎ 913 600 011, ⓦ www.hotellopedevega.com. MAP P.68–69, POCKET MAP H13. With a great location close to the main art galleries, this hotel is a good mid-priced option. Each of the seven floors is dedicated to a theme relating to playwright Lope de Vega, while the business-style rooms are neat and comfortable. **Doubles from €80.**

HOTEL MORA > Paseo del Prado 32 Ⓜ Atocha ☏ 914 201 569, Ⓦ www .hotelmora.com. MAP P.68–69, POCKET MAP H7. A slightly old-fashioned 62-room hotel perfectly positioned for the galleries on the Paseo del Prado. All of the refurbished rooms have a/c and some have pleasant views across the street (double glazing blocks out the worst of the traffic noise). **Doubles from €86.**

HOTEL PALACE > Plaza de las Cortes 7 Ⓜ Sol ☏ 913 608 000, Ⓦ www.westinpalacemadrid.com. MAP P.68–69, POCKET MAP H12–13. Colossal, sumptuous hotel with every imaginable facility but none of the snootiness of you might expect from its aristocratic appearance. A spectacular, glass-covered central patio and luxurious rooms are part of its charm. **Doubles from €235.**

HOTEL VILLA REAL > Plaza de las Cortes 10 Ⓜ Sol ☏ 914 203 767, Ⓦ www.derbyhotels.es. MAP P.68–69, POCKET MAP G12. Aristocratic and highly original, the *Villa Real* comes complete with its own art collection owned by Catalan entrepreneur Jordi Clos. Each of the 96 elegant double rooms has a spacious sitting area (there are several suites too) and many have a balcony overlooking the plaza. The rooftop restaurant, which has some Andy Warhol originals on the wall, affords splendid views down towards the Paseo del Prado. Discount rates start at around €150, although **doubles normally start from €200.**

HOTEL VINCCI SOMA > C/Goya 79 Ⓜ Goya ☏ 914 357 545, Ⓦ www .vinccihoteles.com. MAP P.68–69, POCKET MAP K3. This modern hotel, which is close to the Salamanca shops and Plaza Colón, has a sophisticated feel to it with its tasteful rooms and good service. Internet offers can bring the price down to around €90. **Doubles from €120.**

NH ALCALÁ > C/Alcalá 66 Ⓜ Príncipe de Vergara ☏ 914 351 060, Ⓦ www .nh-hotels.com. MAP P.68–69, POCKET MAP K4. Large, classy hotel belonging to the efficient *NH* chain, just to the north of the Retiro, with smart rooms, professional staff, laundry facilities and a car park. Expensive, but good deals available during the summer and at weekends. Special weekend offers can bring the price down to €70. **Doubles from €110.**

NH PASEO DEL PRADO > Plaza Cánovas del Castillo 4 Ⓜ Banco de España ☏ 914 292 887, Ⓦ www .nh-hotels.com. MAP P.68–69, POCKET MAP H13. A new addition to the hotels in the area, this large, plush member of the *NH Collection* chain is attractively situated in front of the Neptune fountain on the Paseo del Prado. It's not that pricey either, given the excellent facilities and luxurious surroundings. The hotel's restaurant serves some high-class tapas too. There is a slightly cheaper sister hotel, the *NH Nacional*, just up the road at Paseo del Prado 48. **Doubles from €120.**

RADISSON BLU, MADRID PRADO > C/Moratín 52, Plaza de Platería Martínez Ⓜ Atocha ☏ 915 242 626, Ⓦ www.radissonblu.com/pradohotel -madrid. MAP 68–69, POCKET MAP J14. Designer hotel located along the Paseo del Prado featuring sleek rooms in black, brown and white, photos of the Madrid skyline adorning the walls, black slate bathrooms and coffee machines. There is a spa and indoor pool, a whisky bar and a restaurant too. **Doubles from €112.**

Gran Vía, Chueca and Malasaña

HOSTAL SIL/SERRANOS >
C/Fuencarral 95, 2° & 3° Ⓜ Tribunal ☏ 914 488 972, Ⓦ www.silserranos .com. MAP P.82–83, POCKET MAP F2. Two friendly *hostales* located at the quieter end of C/Fuencarral in Malasaña. A variety of simple but comfortable rooms all with a/c, modern bathrooms and TV. Triples and quadruples available. **Doubles from €59.**

HOSTAL ZAMORA > Plaza Vázquez de Mella 1, 4° izqda Ⓜ Gran Vía ☎ 915 217 031, Ⓦ www.hostalzamora .com. MAP P.82–83, POCKET MAP F4. Seventeen simple rooms in an agreeable family-run place, most of which overlook the plaza. All rooms have a/c, modern bathrooms and TV. There are good-value family rooms too. **Doubles from €45.**

HOTEL ABALÚ > C/Pez 19, 1° Ⓜ Noviciado ☎ 915 314 744, Ⓦ www.hotelabalu.com. MAP P.82–83, POCKET MAP E3. This boutique hotel, which is just north of Gran Vía, has vibrant Luis Delgado-designed rooms, each one brimming with individual touches such as mini-chandeliers, butterfly prints and patterned mirrors. Personal service guaranteed. **Doubles from €80.**

HOTEL AROSA > C/Salud 21 Ⓜ Gran Vía ☎ 915 321 600, Ⓦ www .hotelarosa.es. MAP P.82–83, POCKET MAP E4. Right in the heart of town, the *Arosa* has 126 spacious, a/c rooms. The standard rooms are functional, but there are sixteen more expensive oriental-style "zen" rooms with extras such as a plasma TV, free mini-bar, bathrobe and slippers. Some of the surrounding streets are a little down-at-heel, but don't let this put you off. **Doubles from €90.**

HOTEL DE LAS LETRAS > Gran Vía 11 Ⓜ Gran Vía ☎ 915 237 980, Ⓦ www .hoteldelasletras.com. MAP P.82–83, POCKET MAP F10. An elegant design-conscious hotel housed in a lovely early nineteenth-century building at the smarter end of Gran Vía. The stylish, high-ceilinged rooms decorated with literary quotations come complete with plasma TVs. Downstairs there's a smooth bar and lounge area and a high-quality restaurant with reasonably priced dishes. **Doubles from €120.**

HOTEL SAN LORENZO > C/Clavel 8 Ⓜ Gran Vía ☎ 915 213 057, Ⓦ www .hotel-sanlorenzo.com. MAP P.82–83, POCKET MAP F4. A former *hostal* that has been upgraded to a neat and tidy three-star hotel offering clean and comfortable rooms with a/c and

bathrooms. Family rooms also available. **Doubles from €50.**

PETIT PALACE DUCAL > C/Hortaleza 3 Ⓜ Gran Vía ☎ 915 211 043, Ⓦ www .hthoteles.com. MAP P.82–83, POCKET MAP F4. A former *hostal* upgraded and recently refurbished to become one of the *High Tech* chain of hotels. Situated in the heart of Chueca, it has 58 sleek rooms with all manner of mod cons. Stylish **doubles cost around €90**, family rooms around **€130.**

ROOM MATE OSCAR > Plaza Vázquez de Mella 12 Ⓜ Gran Vía ☎ 917 011 173, Ⓦ www.room-matehotels.com. MAP P.82–83, POCKET MAP F4. Part of the hip *Room Mate* chain, this hotel is in the heart of Chueca and popular with the gay community. It has a garish psychedelic lobby, super cool sparkling white bar area, as well as space age, design-conscious rooms and a rooftop splash pool popular for evening cocktails. The restaurant serves up a good €12 *menú del día* and some creative tapas. **Doubles from €80.**

U HOSTEL MADRID > C/Sagasta 22 Ⓜ Alonso Martínez ☎ 914 450 300, Ⓦ www.uhostels.com. MAP P.82–83, POCKET MAP G2. Spacious, comfortable and smart rooms in this sparkling new hostel which sprawls its way over five floors of a renovated building close to the pleasant Plaza Santa Bárbara. Options include en-suite doubles, family suites, quadruples, female dormitories and six-, eight- and twelve-bed dormitories. Other extras include a/c, free wi-fi, a chill-out zone and a €3 breakfast. **Dorm beds from €18, doubles from €60.**

Salamanca & Chamberí

HOSTAL RESIDENCIA DON DIEGO > C/Velázquez 45, 5° Ⓜ Velázquez ☎ 914 350 760, Ⓦ www.hostal dondiego.com. MAP P.92, POCKET MAP K2. Although officially a *hostal*, this comfortable, friendly place situated in an upmarket area of town is more like a hotel. The quiet rooms, with full facilities, a/c and satellite TV, are reasonably priced for the area. Some English-speaking staff. **Doubles from €53.**

HOTEL ORFILA > C/Orfila 6
Ⓜ Alonso Martínez ☎917 027 770, Ⓦwww.hotelorfila.com. MAP P.92, POCKET MAP H2. Transport yourself back in time at this exclusive boutique hotel housed in a beautiful nineteenth-century mansion on a quiet street north of Alonso Martínez. Twelve of the exquisite rooms are suites, there is an elegant terrace for tea and drinks and an upmarket restaurant, too. **Doubles from €200.**

HOTEL SANTO MAURO > C/Zurbano
36 Ⓜ Rubén Darío ☎913 196 900, Ⓦwww.hotelacsantomauro.com. MAP P.92, POCKET MAP H1. This is where the Beckhams first installed themselves when David signed for Real Madrid in 2003 and this former aristocrat's residence has all the luxury and exclusivity you'd expect. Palatial rooms, a restaurant that looks like a gentleman's club, a delightful outdoor terrace and an indoor pool are all part of the package. **Doubles from €250.**

HOTEL ÚNICO > C/Claudio Cuello 67
Ⓜ Serrano ☎917 810 173, Ⓦwww .unicohotelmadrid.com. MAP P.92, POCKET MAP J2. Luxury 44-room boutique-style hotel in a renovated nineteenth-century mansion. Large rooms, bathrooms with power showers, elegant communal areas and a garden terrace. The restaurant (see p.96) is run by distinguished Catalan chef Ramon Frexia. **Doubles from €184.**

PETIT PALACE EMBASSY >
C/Serrano 46 Ⓜ Serrano ☎914 313 060, Ⓦwww.hthotels.com. MAP P.92, POCKET MAP J2. A four-star member of the sleek *High Tech* chain of hotels, close to Plaza Colón and in the middle of the upmarket Salamanca shopping district. The *Embassy* has 75 rooms, including ten family ones for up to four people. Free internet access and flat-screen TVs. **Doubles from €105.**

Plaza de España

CASÓN DEL TORMES > C/Río 7
Ⓜ Plaza de España ☎915 419 746, Ⓦwww.hotelcasondeltormes.com. MAP P.100, POCKET MAP C4. Welcoming three-star place in a quiet street next to Plaza de España. The 63 a/c, en-suite rooms are functional but very comfortable and hotel facilities include a bar and breakfast room, and helpful, English-speaking staff. **Doubles from €64.**

HOSTAL BUENOS AIRES >
Gran Vía 61, 2° Ⓜ Plaza de España ☎915 420 102, Ⓦwww.hoteleshn .com. MAP P.100, POCKET MAP D4. Twenty-five pleasantly decorated rooms with a/c, satellite TV, free wi-fi, modern bathrooms, plus double glazing to keep out much of the noise. **Doubles from €46.**

HOTEL EMPERADOR > Gran Vía 53
Ⓜ Santo Domingo ☎915 472 800, Ⓦwww.emperadorhotel.com. MAP P.100, POCKET MAP D4. The main reason to come here is the stunning rooftop swimming pool with its magnificent views. The hotel itself is geared up for the organized tour market and is rather impersonal, but the rooms are large and well decorated. **Doubles from €90.**

HOTEL SANTO DOMINGO > C/San
Bernardo 1 Ⓜ Santo Domingo ☎915 479 800, Ⓦwww.hotelsanto domingo.es. MAP P.100, POCKET MAP D4. What with the jungle paintings adorning the car park, the private art collection, the hanging garden and the rooftop swimming pool with views over the city, this *Mercure chain* hotel is full of surprises. Rooms have tasteful individual decor, large beds and walk-in shower rooms. **Doubles from €105.**

HOTEL TIROL > C/Marqués de
Urquiqo 4 Ⓜ Argüelles ☎915 481 900, Ⓦwww.t3tirol.com. MAP P.100, POCKET MAP B1. A good option if you are travelling with young children, the *Tirol* provides family rooms with a double bed and bunks or an adjoining kids' room. There is a play area too and the hotel is close to the Parque del Oeste and the teleférico into Casa de Campo. €140–180 for a family of four. **Doubles from €75.**

Arrival

Whatever your point of arrival, it's an easy business getting into the centre of Madrid. The airport is connected by metro, shuttle buses and taxis, while the city's main train and bus stations are all linked to the metro system.

By air

The **Aeropuerto de Barajas** (☏ 913 211 000, ⊛ www.aena.es) is 16km east of the city. It has four terminals, including the vast T4 building designed by Richard Rogers and Carlos Lamela. All Iberia's domestic and international flights, as well as airlines that belong to the Oneworld group, such as British Airways and American Airlines, use T4 (a 10min shuttle bus ride from the other terminals); other international flights and budget airlines, including Aer Lingus, Easyjet and Ryanair, go from T1, while Air France, KLM and SAS use T2.

From the airport, the **metro link** (Line 8) takes you from T4 and T2 to the city's Nuevos Ministerios station in just twelve minutes (daily 6am–2am; €4.50). From there, connecting metro lines take you to city-centre locations in about fifteen minutes. The new Cercanías train line takes you directly from T4 to Chamartín in the north of the city in eleven minutes (daily 6am–12.15am; €2.40).

The route by road to central Madrid is more variable, depending on rush-hour traffic, and can take anything from twenty minutes to an hour. Airport express buses run round the clock from each terminal to Cibeles and Atocha (stops only at Cibeles from 11.30pm–6am; every 15–35min; €5) with a journey time of around forty minutes. Taxis are always available outside, too, and

cost around €25–30 to the centre (including a €5.50 airport supplement), depending on the traffic.

By train

Trains from France and northern Spain (including the high-speed links to Segovia and Valladolid) arrive at the **Estación de Chamartín**, in the north of the city, connected by metro with the centre, and by regular commuter trains (*trenes de cercanías*) to the more central **Estación de Atocha**. Atocha has two interconnected terminals: one for local services; the other for all points in southern and eastern Spain, including the high-speed services to Barcelona, Sevilla, Toledo, Malaga, Valencia, Alicante, Albacete and Zaragoza. For train information and **reservations** call ☏ 902 320 320 or go to ⊛ www.renfe.com.

By bus

Bus terminals are scattered throughout the city, but the largest – used by all of the international bus services – is the **Estación Sur de Autobuses** at c/Méndez Álvaro 83, 1.5km south of Atocha train station (☏ 914 684 200, ⊛ www.estacionde autobuses.com; Ⓜ Méndez Álvaro).

By car

All main roads into Madrid bring you right into the city centre, although eccentric signposting and even more eccentric driving can be unnerving. Both ring roads – the M40 and the M30 – and the Paseo de la Castellana, the main north–south artery, are all notorious bottlenecks, although virtually the whole city centre can be close to gridlock during **rush-hour periods** (Mon–Fri 7.30–9.30am & 6–8.30pm). Be prepared for a long trawl around the streets to find **parking** and even when you find somewhere, in most central areas you'll have to buy a ticket at one of the roadside meters (€2.95 for a maximum stay of two hours in the blue-coloured bays; €2.40 for a maximum stay of one hour in the green-coloured bays; charges apply Mon–Fri 9am–8pm, Sat & Aug 9am–3pm). Another option is to put your car in one of the many signposted parkings (up to €3 for an hour and around €31.50 for a day). Once in the city, and with public transport being both efficient and good value, your own vehicle is really only of use for out-of-town excursions.

Getting around

Madrid is an easy city to get around. The central areas are walkable and going on foot is certainly the best way to appreciate and get to know the city. The metro is clean, modern and efficient, buses are also very good and serve some of the more out-of-the-way districts, while taxis are always available.

The metro

The **metro** (ⓦ www.metromadrid.es) is by far the quickest way of getting around Madrid, serving most places you're likely to want to get to. It runs from 6am until 2am and the flat fare is €1.50 for the central zone stations or €12.20 for a ten-trip ticket (*bono de diez viajes*) which can be used on buses too. The network has undergone massive expansion in recent years and some of the outlying commuter districts are now connected by light railways which link with the existing metro stations (supplement fares for some of these). Lines are numbered and colour-coded, and the direction of travel is indicated by the name of the terminus station. You can pick up a free colour map of the system (*plano del metro*) at any station.

Local trains

The **local train** network, or Cercanías, is the most efficient way of connecting between the main train stations and also provides the best route out to many of the suburbs and nearby towns. Most trains are air-conditioned, fares are cheap and there are good connections with the metro. Services generally run every fifteen to thirty minutes from 6am to around midnight. For more information go to the RENFE website (ⓦ www.renfe.com) and click on the Cercanías section for Madrid.

The tourist travel pass

I f you're using public transport extensively it's worth thinking about getting a **tourist pass** (*abono turístico*) covering the metro, train and bus. These are non-transferable and you'll need to show your passport or identity card at the time of purchase. Zone A cards cover the city of Madrid, Zone T cards cover the whole region including Toledo and Guadalajara but not the airport buses. They are available for a duration of one to seven days and range in cost from €8.40 for a Zone A daily card to €70.80 for a weekly one for Zone T (under-11s are half price, under-4s are free) and can be purchased at all metro stations, the airport and tourist offices. If you are staying longer, passes (*abonos*) covering the metro, train and bus are available for a calendar month.

Buses

The comprehensive **bus network**
(wwww.emtmadrid.es) is a good
way to get around and see the
sights. There are information booths
at Plaza de la Cibeles and Puerta
del Sol, which dispense a huge route
map (*plano de los transportes de
Madrid*) and also sell bus passes.
Fares are the same as the metro,
at €1.50 a journey, or €12.20 for a
ten-trip ticket (*bono de diez viajes*)
which can be used on both forms of
transport. When you get on the bus,
punch your ticket in a machine by
the driver. You can also buy tickets
from the driver, but try and have the
right money.

Services run from 6am to midnight,
with *búho* (owl) buses operating
through the night on twenty routes
around the central area and out to
the suburbs: departures are half-
hourly midnight–5.30am from Plaza
de la Cibeles.

Taxis

Madrid has thousands of reasonably
priced taxis that you can wave down
on the street – look for white cars
with a diagonal red stripe on the side.

Seven or eight euros will get you to
most places within the centre and,
although it's common to round up the
fare, you're not expected to tip. The
minimum fare is €2.30 (€2.35 on Sun
and hols) and supplements (€3–5.50)
are charged for baggage, going to
the airport, train and bus stations or
outside the city limits. To phone for
a taxi, call ☎ 915 478 600 (also for
wheelchair-friendly cabs), 914 051
213, 913 712 131 or 914 473 232.

Bicycles

Madrid is pretty bike-unfriendly,
though a future city hire scheme is
touted. Determined cyclists could
try Calmera, C/Atocha 98 (Mon–Sat
9.30am–1.30pm & 4.30–8pm;
☎ 915 277 574; ⓜ Antón Martín),
and Karacol at C/Tortosa 8 (Mon–Fri
10.30am–2pm & 5.30–8pm, Sat
10.30am–2pm; ☎ 915 399 633;
ⓜ Atocha). For bike tours outside
Madrid get in touch with w bravobike
.com at Juan Alvarez Mendizábal
19 (☎ 915 582 945/607 448 440;
ⓜ Ventura Rodríguez) or w bikespain
.info at Plaza de la Villa 1 (☎ 917 590
653/677 356 586; ⓜ Ópera).

Useful bus routes

#2 From west to east: from Argüelles metro station running along
C/Princesa, past Plaza de España, along Gran Vía, past Cibeles and out past
the Retiro.

#3 From south to north: Puerta de Toledo, through Sol, up towards Gran Vía
and then Alonso Martínez and northwards.

#5 From Sol via Cibeles, Colón and the Paseo de la Castellana to
Chamartín.

#27 From Embajadores, via Atocha, up the length of the Castellana to Plaza
de Castilla.

#33 From Príncipe Pío out via the Puente de Segovia to the Parque de
Atracciones and Zoo in Casa de Campo.

#C1 and C2 The Circular bus route takes a broad circuit round the city from
Atocha, via Puerta de Toledo, Príncipe Pío, Plaza de España, Moncloa, Cuatro
Caminos, Avenida de América and Goya.

City tours

The *turismo* in Plaza Mayor (see p.28) can supply details of guided **English-language walking tours** around the city on the "Descubre Madrid" programme; these cost from €5.90 (info at ⓦ www.esmadrid.com/visitasguiadas; tickets ☎ 902 221 424). For a **bus tour** of all the major sights, hop on at the stop between the Prado and the *Ritz* hotel; tickets cost €21 (children €9, under-6s free) and allow you to jump on and off at various points throughout the city. Pick-up points include Puerta del Sol, Plaza de Colón, Plaza de España and the Palacio Real. For the more adventurous, Madsegs offers a three-hour **segway tour** of the city (March–Oct 10am, Nov–Feb noon; meeting point in Plaza de España; €65 plus €15 deposit; ☎ 659 824 499, ⓦ www.madsegs.com), while GoCar (C/Ferraz 26, near Plaza de España; ☎ 915 594 535, ⓦ www.gocartours.es/madrid; prices start at €35/hr for a two-person car, all day €99) offers tours in little yellow computer-guided storytelling vehicles.

Car rental

See p.132 for more information on driving in Madrid. Major operators have branches at the airport and train stations. Central offices include: Atesa, Atocha ☎ 915 061 846, ⓦ www.atesa.es; Avis, Gran Vía 60 (ⓜ Santo Domingo) ☎ 915 484 204, reservations ☎ 902 180 854, ⓦ www.avisworld.com; Europcar, C/San Leonardo 8 (ⓜ Plaza España) ☎ 915 418 892, ⓦ www.europcar.com; Hertz, Atocha station ☎ 902 023 932, ⓦ www.hertz.com; EasyCar, ⓦ www.easycar.com; Pepecar, near to Atocha and Chamartín stations ☎ 807 414 243, ⓦ www.pepecar.com.

Directory A-Z

Addresses

Calle (street) is abbreviated to C/ in addresses, followed by the number on the street, then another number that indicates the floor, eg c/Arenal 23, 5° means fifth floor of no. 23 Arenal Street. You may also see *izquierda* and *derecha*, meaning (apartment or office) left or right of the staircase.

Cinema

Madrileños love going to the cinema (*cine*) and, though most foreign films are dubbed into Spanish, a number of cinemas have original-language screenings, listed in a separate *versión original* (v.o.)/*subtitulada* section in the newspapers. Tickets cost €7–9 but most cinemas have a *día del espectador* (usually Mon or Wed) with a reduced admission charge. Be warned that on Sunday night what seems like half of Madrid goes to the movies and queues can be long. The most central cinemas showing v.o. films include the two Renoirs at C/Martín de los Heros 12 and C/Princesa 5, and Golem at C/Martín de los Heros 14, all next to Plaza de España, and the nine-screen Ideal Yelmo Complex, C/Doctor Cortezo 6, south off C/Atocha and near Plaza Santa Ana (ⓜ Sol).

> For the police, medical services and the fire brigade, call ☎ 112.

Crime

Central Madrid is so densely populated – and so busy at just about every hour of the day and night – that it seems to carry very little "big city" threat. However, that's not to say that crime is not a problem, nor that there aren't any sleazy areas to be avoided. Tourists in Madrid, as everywhere, are prime targets for pickpockets and petty thieves so take care of belongings in crowded areas, on buses, in the metro, burger bars and in the Rastro. Be aware also that although the city council has taken steps to combat the problem, the main routes through Casa de Campo and the Parque del Oeste are still frequented by prostitutes and are best steered clear of at night. Calle Montera, near Sol, and some streets just north of Gran Vía are also affected.

Electricity

220 volts. Plugs are two round pins.

Embassies and consulates

Australia, Torre Espacio, Paseo de la Castellana 259D (☎ 913 536 600, ⓦ www.spain.embassy.gov.au; Ⓜ Begoña); Britain, Torre Espacio, Paseo de la Castellana 259D (☎ 913 342 194, ⓦ www.ukinspain.fco .gov.uk; Ⓜ Begoña); Canada, Torre Espacio, Paseo de la Castellana 259D (☎ 913 828 400, ⓦ www.canadainter national.gc.ca); Ⓜ Begoña); Ireland, Paseo de la Castellana 46 (☎ 914 364 093, ⓦ www.embassyofireland. es; Ⓜ Rubén Darío); New Zealand, C/ Pinar 7, 3º (☎ 915 230 226, ⓦ www .nzembassy.com/spain; Ⓜ Gregorio Marañon); US, C/Serrano 75 (☎ 915 872 200, ⓦ www.embusa.es; Ⓜ Rubén Darío); South Africa, C/ Claudio Coello 91 (☎ 914 363 780, ⓦ www.dirco.gov.za/madrid; Ⓜ Rubén Darío).

Gay and lesbian travellers

The main gay organization in Madrid is Coordinadora Gay de Madrid, C/Puebla 9 (Mon–Fri 10am–2pm & 5–8pm; ☎ 915 230 070, ⓦ www.cogam.org), which can give information on health, leisure and gay rights. Feminist and lesbian groups are based at the Centro de la Mujer, C/Barquillo 44, 1º izda (☎ 913 193 689; Ⓜ Chueca). For a good one-stop shop with lots of info on the gay scene, try Berkana Bookshop, C/Hortaleza 64 (Mon–Sat 10.30am–9pm; Sun noon–2pm & 5–9pm; ⓦ www.libreriaberkana.com; Ⓜ Chueca).

Health

Health centres are scattered throughout the city and open 24 hours: one of the most central is at Carrera San Jerónimo 32 (☎ 913 690 491; Ⓜ Sevilla). Central hospitals include El Clínico San Carlos, C/ Profesor Martín Lagos s/n (☎ 913 303 000; Ⓜ Islas Filipinas); Hospital Gregorio Marañon, C/Dr Esquerdo 46 (☎ 915 868 000; Ⓜ O'Donnell); Ciudad Sanitaria La Paz, Paseo de la Castellana 261 (☎ 917 277 000, Ⓜ Begoña). English-speaking doctors are available at the Anglo-American Medical Unit, C/Conde de Aranda 1 (☎ 914 351 823; Mon–Fri 9am–8pm, Sat 10am–3pm; Ⓜ Retiro). The Clinica Dental Plaza Prosperidad at Plaza Prosperidad 3, 2ºB (☎ 914 158 197, ⓦ www.clinicadentalplazaprosperidad .com; Ⓜ Prosperidad) has some English-speaking dentists as does the Clinica Dental Cisne at C/Magallanes 18 (☎ 914 463 221; Ⓜ Quevedo). The following **pharmacies** (distinguished by a green cross) are open 24 hours: C/Mayor 59 (☎ 915 480 014; Ⓜ Sol); C/Toledo 46 (☎ 913 653 458; Ⓜ La Latina); C/Atocha 46 (☎ 913 692 000; Ⓜ Antón Martín); C/Goya 12 (☎ 915 754 924; Ⓜ Serrano).

Internet

There are free wi-fi hotspots at many newspaper stands in the city and on buses, while the city centre is peppered with *locutorios* that provide internet. The *Workcenter* venues on Plaza Canalejas (Mon–Fri 8am–9pm, Sat & Sun 10am–2.30pm & 5–8.30pm; ☎ 913 601 395; Ⓜ Sevilla) and at C/Alberto Aguilera 1 (Ⓜ San Bernardo; open 24hr) have well-equipped internet cafés. *Café Comercial* on the Glorieta de Bilbao has an internet café upstairs. Prices range from €1 to €3.50 per hour.

Left luggage

There are left-luggage facilties (*consignas*) at Barajas Airport in terminals 1, 2 and 4 (open 24hr; €5.80/day); the Estación Sur bus station; and lockers at Atocha (open 5.30am–10.15pm; €3.60–5.20/day) and Chamartín (open 7am–11pm; €3.60–5.20/day) train stations.

Lost property

For lost property ring the municipal depot on ☎ 915 279 590 at Paseo del Molino 7 (open Mon–Fri 9am–2pm; Ⓜ Legazpi); bring ID. For property left in a taxi call ☎ 914 804 613; on a bus call ☎ 902 507 850; on the metro call ☎ 917 212 957.

Money

Banks are plentiful throughout the city and are the best places to change money. Opening hours are normally Mon–Fri 9am–2pm. Branches of El Corte Inglés have exchange offices with long hours and reasonably competitive rates; the most central is on C/Preciados, close to Puerta del Sol. Barajas Airport also has a 24 hour currency exchange office. The rates at the exchange bureaux scattered around the city are often very poor, though they don't usually charge commission. ATM cash machines (*cajeros automáticos*) are widespread and accept most credit and debit cards. Credit cards are widely accepted in hotels, restaurants and shops.

Opening hours

Smaller shops generally open 10am–2pm and 5–8pm Mon–Fri, but only open in the mornings on Sat. Department stores and chains tend not to close for lunch and open all day Sat; larger ones open on the first Sun of the month too (except in Aug). Stores in the tourist zones in the centre also open on Sun. Restaurants generally serve from 1.30–4pm and 8.30pm–midnight, with many closing for a rest day on Mon. Bars stay open till the early hours – usually around 2am – while clubs close around 5am, depending on the licence they hold. Museums close on Jan 1, Jan 6, May 1, Dec 24 and 31.

Phones

International calls can be made from any phone box or *locutorio* (call centre). The latter are plentiful in the centre and often cheaper than phone boxes. Phones accept either coins or phonecards that cost €5, €10, €15 and €20, available from post offices or *estancos* (see p.138). Calling Madrid from abroad, dial your international access code, then 34, followed by the subscriber's number which will nearly always start with 91. Mobile phone users from the UK should be able to use their phones in Spain – check with your service provider before leaving about costs. Many American cellphones do not work with the Spanish mobile network. For national directory enquiries ring ☎ 11818; for international enquiries call ☎ 11825.

Post offices

Centrally located post offices are at Paseo del Prado 1 and in El Corte Inglés, C/Preciados 3 (ⓜSol) and there's another with extended hours at C/Mejía Lequerica 7 (ⓜAlonso Martínez). Buy stamps (*sellos*) at *estancos*.

Public holidays

The main national holidays are: Jan 1 (Año Nuevo); Jan 6 (Reyes); Easter Thursday (Jueves Santo); Good Friday (Viernes Santo); May 1 (Fiesta del Trabajo); May 2 (Día de la Comunidad); May 15 (San Isidro); Aug 15 (Virgen de la Paloma); Oct 12 (Día de la Hispanidad); Nov 1 (Todos Los Santos); Nov 9 (Virgen de la Almudena); Dec 6 (Día de la Constitución); Dec 8 (La Inmaculada); Dec 25 (Navidad).

Smoking

Smoking is banned in all bars, restaurants and clubs, though it is common on outdoor *terrazas*.

Swimming pools and aquaparks

The Piscina Canal Isabel II, Avda de Filipinas 54 (daily 10am–8.30pm; ⓜRíos Rosas), is a large outdoor swimming pool, and the best central option. Alternatively, try the open-air *piscina* in the Casa de Campo (daily 10am–8.30pm; ⓜLago). There are also a number of aquaparks around the city, the closest being Aquópolis de San Fernando (ⓦwww.san-fernando .aquopolis.es), 16km out on the N-II Barcelona road (buses #221, #224A and #226 from the intercambiador at Arda de América). Outside May–Sept most outdoor pools are closed.

Ticket agencies

For theatre and concert tickets try: Atrapalo ☏902 200 808, ⓦwww .atrapalo.com; ⓦwww.entradas.com; Caixa de Catalunya/Tele Entrada ☏902 101 212, ⓦwww.telentrada .com; El Corte Inglés ☏902 400 222, ⓦwww.elcorteingles.es; FNAC ☏915 956 100; and Ticketmaster ⓦwww.ticketmaster.es. The booth at Plaza del Carmen 1 near Sol (*taquilla último minuto*) sells last-minute tickets to a variety of events (Wed, Thurs, Sun 5–8pm, Fri & Sat 5–10pm; ⓦwww.taquillaultimominuto.com).

Time

Madrid is one hour ahead of Greenwich Mean Time during winter and two hours ahead from March–Oct. Clocks go forward in late March and back an hour in late Oct.

Tipping

When tipping, adding around five to ten percent to a restaurant bill is acceptable but rarely more than €5, while in bars and taxis, rounding up to the nearest euro is the norm.

Tourist information and passes

The chief tourist offices are at the following locations: Barajas International Airport T1 & T4; T1 (Mon–Sat 8am–8pm, Sun 9am–2pm; ☏913 058 656); T4 (daily 9.30am–8.30pm; ☏913 338 248); Colón (daily 9.30am–8.30pm; ☏915 881 636; ⓜColón); Palacio de Cibeles (Tues–Sun 10am–8pm; ⓜBanco de España); Estación de Atocha (Mon–Fri 9am–8pm, Sat & Sun 9am–1pm; ☏913 159 976; ⓜAtocha Renfe); Estación de Chamartín (Mon–Fri 8am–8pm, Sat 9am–2pm; ☏913 159 976; ⓜChamartín); Plaza Mayor 27 (daily 9.30am–8.30pm; ☏915 881 636; ⓜSol). These are supplemented by booths near the Prado, the Reina Sofia and in Plaza del Callao off Gran Vía (daily 9.30am–8.30pm). The Madrid tourist board has a comprehensive website at ⓦwww.esmadrid .com, while the regional one has one covering the whole of the province at ⊚ www.turismomadrid.es. You can phone for tourist information in English on ☎ 902 100 007, a premium-rate number that links all the regional tourist offices mentioned below, and on ☎ 915 881 636.

Listings information is in plentiful supply in Madrid. The newspapers *El País* (⊚ www.elpais.es) and *El Mundo* (⊚ www.metropoli.com) have excellent daily listings (in Spanish), and on Friday both publish sections devoted to events, bars and restaurants. If your time in Madrid doesn't coincide with the Friday supplements, or you want a full rundown, pick up the weekly **listings magazine** *La Guía del Ocio* (⊚ www.guiadelocio.com; €1) at any newsagent's stand. The *ayuntamiento* (city council) also publishes a monthly what's-on magazine, *esMadrid* (in English and Spanish), free from any of the tourist offices. Finally, *In Madrid* (⊚ www.in-madrid.com) is a free monthly English-language paper, available in bars, that features useful reviews of nightlife.

The Madrid **tourist card** (☎ 902 877 996, ⊚ www.madridcard .com and www.neotourism.com) gives the holder admission to over fifty museums and sights, a tour of the Bernabéu, the teleférico, a guided walk of the old city, plus discounts at some shops and restaurants. It costs €44 for one day (€54 for two, €64 for three) and is on sale online and at the Plaza Mayor tourist office (see opposite). Do your sums before you splash out though, as you need to cram a lot into a day's sightseeing to get your money's worth and if you want to concentrate on the big three art galleries, the Paseo del Arte ticket (see p.70) is better value.

Theatre

Madrid has a vibrant theatre scene which, if you speak the language, is worth sampling. You can catch anything from Lope de Vega to contemporary productions, and there's a good range on offer during the annual Festival de Otoño (Sept–Nov). For current productions, check the listings sources above.

Travelling with children

Although many of Madrid's main sights may lack children-specific activities, there's still plenty to keep kids occupied during a short stay, from various parks – including the Retiro (see p.72) – to swimming pools (see opposite) and the zoo (see p.104). There is also an ecological theme park/zoo on the outskirts of the city (⊚ www.faunia .es). Children are doted on in Spain and welcome in nearly all cafés and restaurants.

Travellers with disabilities

Madrid is not particularly well geared up for disabled visitors (*minus-válidos*), although the situation is improving. The Organizacíon Nacional de Ciegos de España (ONCE; National Organization for the Blind, C/Prim 3 (☎ 915 325 000, ⊚ www.once.es; ⓜ Chueca) provides specialist advice, as does the Federación de Asocia-ciones de Minusválidos Físicos de la Comunidad de Madrid (FAMMA) at C/Galileo 69 (☎ 915 933 550, ⊚ www .famma.org; ⓜ Islas Filipinas). ⊚ www.discapnet.es is a useful source of information (Spanish only). Wheelchair-accessible taxis can be ordered from Eurotaxi (☎ 630 026 478 or 687 924 027) and Radio Taxi (☎ 915 478 200 or 915 478 600).

Festivals and events

As well as these festivals, check out the **cultural events** organized by the city council, in particular the Veranos de la Villa (July–Sept) and Festival de Otoño (Sept–Nov), which include music concerts, theatre and cinema. There are annual festivals for alternative theatre (Feb), flamenco (Feb), books (end of May), dance (April–May), photography (mid-June to mid-July) and jazz (Nov). See ⓦ www.esmadrid.com.

CABALGATA DE LOS REYES

January 5

A celebration of the arrival of the gift-bearing Three Kings, the evening of January 5 sees a procession through the centre of Madrid in which children are showered with sweets.

CARNAVAL

The week before Lent

Partying and fancy-dress parades, especially in the gay zone around Chueca. The end of Carnaval is marked by the bizarre parade, El Entierro de la Sardina (The Burial of the Sardine), on Paseo de la Florida.

SEMANA SANTA

Easter week is celebrated with a series of solemn processions around Madrid, with Jueves Santo (Maundy Thursday) and Viernes Santo (Good Friday) both public holidays in the city.

FIESTA DEL DOS DE MAYO

May 2

Celebrations around Madrid, but particularly in Malasaña, are held to commemorate the city's uprising against the French in 1808. The main festive focus is Plaza Dos de Mayo.

FIESTAS DE SAN ISIDRO

May 15, for a week.

Evenings start out with traditional chotis, music and dancing, and bands play each night in the Jardines de las Vistillas (south of the Palacio Real). The fiestas mark the start of the bullfighting season.

LA FERIA DEL LIBRO

End of May

Madrid's great book fair takes place with stands set up in the Retiro Park.

GAY PRIDE WEEK

End of June or beginning of July

Gay Pride is a week-long party in Chueca culminating in a parade that brings the city centre to a standstill.

CASTIZO FIESTAS

August 6 to 15

Madrileños put on traditional fiestas to celebrate the saints' days of San Cayetano, San Lorenzo and La Virgen de la Paloma. Much of the activity centres around C/Toledo, Plaza de la Paja and the Jardines de las Vistillas.

NAVIDAD

The Christmas period in Madrid sees Plaza Mayor taken over by a model of a Nativity crib and a large seasonal market with stalls selling all manner of festive decorations.

NOCHE VIEJA

Dec 31

Puerta del Sol is the customary place to gather for midnight, waiting for the strokes of the clock and then attempting to swallow a grape on each strike to bring good luck in the coming year.

Chronology

800s > Muslims establish a defensive outpost on the escarpment above the Manzanares river. It becomes known as "mayrit" – the place of many springs – successively modified to Magerit and then Madrid.

1086 > Madrid taken by the Christians under Alfonso VI, but it remains a relatively insignificant backwater.

1561 > Felipe II chooses Madrid as a permanent home for the court because of its position in the centre of the recently unified Spain. The population surges with the arrival of the royal entourage, and there is a boom in the building industry.

1700–1746 > With the emergence of the Bourbon dynasty under Felipe V, a touch of French style, including the sumptuous Palacio Real, is introduced into the capital.

1759–88 > Carlos III tries to make the city into a home worthy of the monarchy. Streets are cleaned up, sewers and street lighting installed, and work begins on the Museo del Prado.

1795–1808 > Spain falls under the influence of Napoleonic France, with their troops entering the capital in 1808. The heavily out-gunned Madrileños are defeated in a rising on May 2 and Napoleon installs his brother Joseph on the throne.

1812–14 > The French are removed by a combined Spanish and British army and the monarchy makes a return under the reactionary Fernando VII.

1833–1875 > Spanish society is riven with divisions which explode into a series of conflicts known as the Carlist Wars and lead to chronic political instability, including a brief period as a republic.

1875–1900 > Madrid undergoes significant social changes prompted by a rapid growth in population and the emergence of a working class. The socialist party, the PSOE, is founded in the city in 1879.

1923–1931 > A hard-line military regime under Miguel Primo de Rivera takes control, with King Alfonso XIII relegated to the background. The king eventually decides to abdicate in 1931, and the Second Republic is ushered in.

1936–39 > The Right grows increasingly restless and a group of army generals organize an uprising in July 1936 which ignites the Spanish Civil War. Madrid resists and becomes a Republican stronghold.

1939 > Franco and his victorious Nationalists enter the city. Mass reprisals take place and Franco installs himself in the country residence of El Pardo.

1939–1953 > Spain endures yet more suffering during the post-war years until a turnaround in American policy rehabilitates Franco, as the US searches for anti-Communist Cold War allies.

1970s > Franco eventually dies in November 1975. He is succeeded by King Juan Carlos who presides over the transition to democracy.

1981 > In a last-gasp attempt to re-establish itself, the military under Colonel Tejero storms the parliament in Madrid, but a lack of support from the king and army cause its collapse. The Socialists led by Felipe González win the 1982 elections.

1980s > Freedom from the shackles of dictatorship and the release of long-pent-up creative forces help create La Movida, with Madrid becoming the epicentre of the movement.

1990s > The Socialists become increasingly discredited as they are entangled in a web of scandal and corruption, losing control of Madrid in 1991 and the country in 1996 to the conservative Partido Popular (PP).

1992 > Madrid was named European Capital of Culture.

2004 > The March 11 bombings carried out by Muslim extremists at Atocha train station kill 191 and injure close to 2000. The Socialists return to power in the general elections which follow, although the PP remain firmly in control of the local government.

2004–08 > Madrid fails in its bids for the 2012 and 2016 Olympics, losing out to London and then Rio de Janeiro. High-profile building projects such as the Richard Rogers airport terminal, Norman Foster's Torre Caja Madrid skyscraper, Rafael Moneo's Prado extension and the M30 ring road 6-km long mega-tunnel are all completed before the onset of the recession and the end of the property boom.

2008–present > The effects of the global economic crisis combined with the endemic problems of property speculation, profligate spending on showcase projects and corruption mean the crisis hits Spain even harder. The centre-right Popular Party is returned to power in the 2011 general election. Unemployment reaches record highs, the economy flatlines in terms of growth and corruption scandals continue to plague the country.

Spanish

Once you get into it, Spanish is one of the easiest languages around, and people are eager to try and understand even the most faltering attempt. English is spoken at the main tourist attractions, but you'll get a far better reception if you try communicating with Madrileños in their own tongue.

Pronunciation

The rules of pronunciation are pretty straightforward and strictly observed.

A somewhere between the A sound of back and that of father.

E as in get.

I as in police.

O as in hot.

U as in rule.

C is spoken like a TH before E and I, hard otherwise: *cerca* is pronounced "thairka".

G is a guttural H sound (like the ch in loch) before E or I, a hard G elsewhere – *gigante* becomes "higante".

H is always silent.

J is the same as a guttural G: *jamón* is "hamon".

LL sounds like an English Y: *tortilla* is pronounced "torteeya".

N is as in English unless it has a tilde (accent) over it, when it becomes NY: *mañana* sounds like "manyana".

QU is pronounced like an English K.

R is rolled when it is at the start of a word, RR doubly so.

V sounds more like B, *vino* becoming "beano".

X has an S sound before consonants, normal X before vowels.

Z is the same as a soft C, so *cerveza* becomes "thairbaytha".

Words and phrases

BASICS

yes, no, ok	sí, no, vale
please, thank you	por favor, gracias
where?, when?	¿dónde?, ¿cuándo?
what?, how much?	¿qué?, ¿cuánto?
here, there	aquí, allí
this, that	esto, eso
now, later	ahora, más tarde
open, closed	abierto/a, cerrado/a
with, without	con, sin
good, bad	buen(o)/a, mal(o)/a
big, small	gran(de), pequeño/a
cheap, expensive	barato, caro
hot, cold	caliente, frío
more, less	más, menos
today, tomorrow	hoy, mañana
yesterday	ayer
the bill	la cuenta
price	precio
free	gratis

GREETINGS AND RESPONSES

hello, goodbye	hola, adiós
good morning	buenos días
good afternoon/ night	buenas tardes/ noches
see you later	hasta luego
sorry	lo siento/disculpe
excuse me	con permiso/perdón
How are you?	¿Cómo está (usted)?
I (don't) understand	(no) entiendo
not at all/you're welcome	de nada
Do you speak english?	¿Habla (usted) inglés?
I (don't) speak Spanish	(no) hablo español
My name is...	Me llamo...
What's your name?	¿Cómo se llama usted?
I am English/ Scottish/ Welsh/ Australian/ Canadian/ American/ Irish/ New Zealander	Soy inglés(a)/ escocés(a)/ galés(a)/ australiano(a)/ canadiense/ americano(a)/ irlandés(a)/ neozelandés(a)

HOTELS, TRANSPORT AND DIRECTIONS

I want	Quiero
I'd like	Quisiera
Do you know...?	¿Sabe....?

I don't know	No sé
Give me (one like that)	Deme (uno así)
Do you have...?	¿Tiene...?
the time	la hora
two beds/double bed	dos camas/cama matrimonial
with shower/bath	con ducha/baño
it's for one person	es para una persona
for one night	para una noche
for one week	para una semana
how do I get to...?	¿por dónde se va a....?
left, right, straight on	izquierda, derecha, todo recto
Where is the bus station/post office/toilet?	¿Dónde está la estación de autobuses/la oficina de correos/el baño?
What's this in Spanish?	¿Cómo se dice en español?
Where does the bus to... leave from?	¿De dónde sale el autobús para...?
I'd like a (return) ticket to...	quisiera un billete (de ida y vuelta) para...
What time does it leave?	¿a qué hora sale?

MONEY

How much?	¿Cuánto es?
I would like to change some money	Me gustaría cambiar dinero
ATM cash machine	cajero automático
foreign exchange bureau	la oficina de cambio
credit card	tarjeta de crédito
travellers' cheques	cheques de viaje

NUMBERS/DAYS/MONTHS/ SEASONS

1	un/uno/una
2	dos
3	tres
4	cuatro
5	cinco
6	seis
7	siete
8	ocho
9	nueve

10	diez
11	once
12	doce
13	trece
14	catorce
15	quince
16	dieciséis
17	diecisiete
18	dieciocho
19	diecinueve
20	veinte
21	veintiuno
30	treinta
40	cuarenta
50	cincuenta
60	sesenta
70	setenta
80	ochenta
90	noventa
100	cien(to)
101	ciento uno
200	doscientos
500	quinientos
1000	mil
Monday	lunes
Tuesday	martes
Wednesday	miércoles
Thursday	jueves
Friday	viernes
Saturday	sábado
Sunday	domingo
today	hoy
yesterday	ayer
tomorrow	mañana
January	enero
February	febrero
March	marzo
April	abril
May	mayo
June	junio
July	julio
August	agosto
September	septiembre
October	octubre
November	noviembre
December	diciembre
spring	primavera
summer	verano
autumn	otoño
winter	invierno

Food and drink

BASICS

aceite	oil
agua	water
ajo	garlic
arroz	rice
azúcar	sugar
huevos	eggs
mantequilla	butter
miel	honey
pan	bread
pimienta	pepper
pinchos/pintxos	a small bite-sized tapa
queso	cheese
sal	salt
sopa	soup
tapa	small serving of food
vinagre	vinegar

MEALS

almuerzo/comida	lunch
botella	bottle
carta	menu
cena	dinner
comedor	dining room
cuchara	spoon
cuchillo	knife
desayuno	breakfast
menú (del día)	daily set-lunch
menú de degustación	set menu offering a taste of several house specialities
mesa	table
platos combinados	mixed plate
ración	a plateful of food
tenedor	fork
vaso	glass

MEAT

albóndigas	meatballs
callos	tripe
caracoles	snails
chorizo	spicy sausage
conejo	rabbit
cochinillo	roast suckling pig
hígado	liver
jamón serrano	cured ham
jamón de york	regular ham
morcilla	black pudding
pollo	chicken
salchicha	sausage

SEAFOOD

ahumados	smoked fish
almejas	clams
anchoas	anchovies
atún	tuna
a la marinera	seafood cooked with garlic, onions and white wine
bacalao	cod
bonito	tuna
boquerones	small, anchovy-like fish, usually served in vinegar
calamares	squid
cangrejo	crab
champiñones	mushrooms
gambas	prawns
langostinos	langoustines
mejillones	mussels
ostras	oysters
pulpo	octopus

FRUIT AND VEGETABLES

aceitunas	olives
alcachofas	artichokes
berenjena	aubergine/eggplant
cebolla	onion
cerezas	cherries
coliflor	cauliflower
ensalada	salad
fresa	strawberry
granada	pomegranate
habas	broad/fava beans
higos	figs
lechuga	lettuce
lentejas	lentils
limón	lemon
manzana	apple
melocotones	peaches
nabos	turnips
naranja	orange
pepino	cucumber
pimientos	peppers

pimientos de padrón	small peppers, with the odd hot one thrown in
piña	pineapple
pisto	assortment of cooked vegetables (like ratatouille)
plátano	banana
pomelo	grapefruit
puerros	leeks
puré	thick soup
repollo	cabbage
sandía	watermelon
setas	oyster mushrooms
tomate	tomato
uvas	grapes
zanahoria	carrot

SPECIALITIES

bocadillo	French-loaf sandwich
cocido	meat and chickpea stew
croquetas	croquettes, with bits of ham in
empanada	slices of fish/ meat pie
ensaladilla	Russian salad (diced vegetables in mayonnaise, often with tuna)
patatas alioli	potatoes in garlic mayonnaise
patatas bravas	fried potatoes in spicy tomato sauce
tortilla (española)	potato omelette
tortilla francesa	plain omelette

tostas	toasted bread with a topping

COOKING METHODS

al ajillo	with olive oil and garlic
a la parilla	charcoal-grilled
a la plancha	grilled on a hot plate
a la romana	fried in batter
al horno	baked in the oven
asado	roast
frito	fried

DESSERTS

arroz con leche	rice pudding
crema catalana	Catalan crème brûlée
cuajada	cream-based dessert often served with honey
flan	crème caramel
helado	ice cream
melocotón en almíbar	peaches in syrup
membrillo	quince paste
nata	whipped cream
natillas	custard
yogur	yoghurt

DRINKS

anís	aniseed liqueur
café (con leche)	(white) coffee
cerveza	beer
té	tea
vino (blanco/rosado/ tinto)	(white/rosé/red) wine
zumo	juice

Glossary

alameda park or grassy promenade

alcázar Moorish fortified palace

avenida avenue (usually abbreviated to avda)

ayuntamiento town hall or council

azulejo glazed ceramic tilework

barrio suburb or neighbourhood

bodega cellar or wine bar

calle (usually abbreviated to C/) street or road

capilla mayor chapel containing the high altar

capilla real royal chapel

castillo castle

cervecería bar specializing in beers

correos post office

corrida bullfight

cuadrilla a bullfighter's team of assistants

edificio building

ermita hermitage

estanco small shop selling stamps and tobacco, recognizable by the brown and yellow signs bearing the word *tabacos*

iglesia church

lonja stock exchange building

marisquería seafood restaurant

mercado market

mesón an old-style restaurant

mirador viewing point

Movida late Seventies/early Eighties creative explosion in Madrid, viewed as Spain's Swinging Sixties

Mudéjar Muslim Spaniard subject to medieval Christian rule, but retaining Islamic worship; most commonly a term applied to architecture which includes buildings built by Moorish craftsmen for the Christian rulers and later designs influenced by Moors. The 1890s to 1930s saw a Mudéjar revival, blended with Art Nouveau and Art Deco forms

museo museum

palacio aristocratic mansion

parador state-run hotel, usually housed in a building of historic interest

patio inner courtyard

Plateresque elaborately decorative Renaissance style, the sixteenth-century successor of Isabelline forms. Named for its resemblance to silversmiths' work (plateria)

plaza square

plaza de toros bullring

posada old name for an inn

puerta gateway

puerto port

sidrería bar specializing in cider

terraza summer outdoor bar

oficina de turismo tourist office

zarzuela light opera

PUBLISHING INFORMATION

This second edition published February 2014 by **Rough Guides Ltd**

80 Strand, London WC2R 0RL

11, Community Centre, Panchsheel Park, New Delhi 110017, India

Distributed by the Penguin Group

Penguin Books Ltd, 80 Strand, London WC2R 0RL

Penguin Group (USA) 345 Hudson Street, NY 10014, USA

Penguin Group (Australia) 250 Camberwell Road, Camberwell, Victoria 3124, Australia

Penguin Group (NZ) 67 Apollo Drive, Mairangi Bay, Auckland 1310, New Zealand

Penguin Group (South Africa) Block D, Rosebank Office Park, 181 Jan Smuts Avenue,

Parktown North, Gauteng, South Africa 2193

Rough Guides is represented in Canada by

Tourmaline Editions Inc., 662 King Street West, Suite 304, Toronto, Ontario, M5V 1M7

Typeset in Minion and Din to an original design by Henry Iles and Dan May.

Printed and bound in China

© Simon Baskett 2014

Maps © Rough Guides except Madrid Metro map © Metro de Madrid S.A. 2013

160pp includes index

A catalogue record for this book is available from the British Library

ISBN 978-1-40933-959-5

3 5 7 9 8 6 4 2

ROUGH GUIDES CREDITS

Text editors: Lucy White and Neil McQuillian

Layout: Nikhil Agarwal and Anita Singh

Cartography: Ed Wright and Katie Bennett

Picture editors: Wilf Matos, Nicole Newman and Tim Draper

Photographers: Lydia Evans and Tim Draper

Production: Linda Dare

Proofreader: Jennifer Speake

Cover design: Wilf Matos and Anita Singh

THE AUTHOR

Simon Baskett lives and works in Madrid with his wife, Trini, and two children Patrick and Laura. He
is a long-suffering Atlético Madrid fan, and has not yet given up hope that he might live long enough
to see them do "the double" once more. His ambition is to win El Gordo (the huge Christmas lottery)
and retire to a local bar.

ACKNOWLEDGEMENTS

Special thanks to Trini once again for all her hard work and patience. Thanks, too, go to Antonio and Javier of the *Hostal Gonzalo*, and to the Metro de Madrid.

HELP US UPDATE

We've gone to a lot of effort to ensure that the second edition of the **Pocket Rough Guide Madrid** is accurate and up-to-date. However, things change – places get "discovered", opening hours are notoriously fickle, restaurants and rooms raise prices or lower standards. If you feel we've got it wrong or left something out, we'd like to know, and if you can remember the address, the price, the hours, the phone number, so much the better.

Please send your comments with the subject line "**Pocket Rough Guide Madrid Update**" to ✉ mail@roughguides.com. We'll credit all contributions and send a copy of the next edition (or any other Rough Guide if you prefer) for the very best emails.

Find more travel information, connect with fellow travellers and book your trip on ⓦ www .roughguides.com

PHOTO CREDITS

Index

Maps are marked in **bold**.

OVER 300 DESTINATIONS

ANDORRA Spain
ANTIGUA The Caribbean
ARGENTINA Argentina, Buenos Aires, South America on a Budget
AUSTRALIA Australia, Australia Map, East Coast Australia, Melbourne, Sydney, Tasmania
AUSTRIA Austria, Europe on a Budget, Vienna
BAHAMAS The Bahamas, The Caribbean
BARBADOS The Caribbean
BELGIUM Belgium & Luxembourg, Brussels
BELIZE Belize, Central America On a Budget, Guetemala & Belize Map
BENIN West Africa
BOLIVIA Bolivia, South America on a Budget
BRAZIL Brazil, Rio, South America on a Budget
BRUNEI Malaysia, Singapore & Brunei [1 title], South East Asia on a Budget
BULGARIA Bulgaria, Europe on a Budget
BURKINA FASO West Africa
CAMBODIA Cambodia, South East Asia on a Budget, Vietnam
CAMEROON West Africa
CANADA Canada, Toronto, Toronto Map, Vancouver
CAPE VERDE West Africa
CARIBBEAN The Caribbean
CHILE Chile, South America on a Budget
CHINA Beijing, China, Hong Kong & Macau, Shanghai
COLOMBIA South America on a Budget
COSTA RICA Central America on a Budget, Costa Rica
CROATIA Croatia, Croatia Map, Europe on a Budget
CUBA Cuba, Cuba Map, Havana, The Caribbean
CYPRUS Cyprus
CZECH REPUBLIC The Czech Republic, Czech Republic Map, Europe on a Budget, Prague, Prague Map, Prague Pocket
DENMARK Copenhagen, Denmark, Europe on a Budget, Scandinavia
DOMINICAN REPUBLIC Dominican Republic, Dominican Republic Map, The Caribbean
ECUADOR Ecuador, South America on a Budget
EGYPT Egypt, Cairo & The Pyramids
EL SALVADOR Central America on a Budget

ENGLAND Britain, Camping, Devon & Cornwall, The Cotswolds, Dorset, Hampshire & The Isle of Wight [1 title], England, Europe on a Budget, The Lake District, London, London Pocket, London Map, London Mini Guide, Walks in London & Southeast England, Yorkshire
ESTONIA Europe on a Budget, Estonia, Latvia & Lithuania [1 title]
FIJI Fiji
FINLAND Europe on a Budget, Finland, Scandinavia
FRANCE Brittany & Normandy, Brittany Map, Corsica, Corsica Map, The Dordogne & the Lot, Europe on a Budget, France, Languedoc & Roussillon, The Loire Valley, Paris, Paris Mini Guide, Paris Pocket, Provence & the Cote d'Azur
FRENCH GUIANA South America on a Budget
GAMBIA West Africa
GERMANY Berlin, Europe on a Budget, Germany
GHANA West Africa
GIBRALTAR Spain
GREECE Athens Map, Athens Pocket, Crete, Crete Map, Europe on a Budget, Greece, Greek Islands
GUATEMALA Central America on a Budget, Guatemala, Guatemala & Belize Map
GUINEA West Africa
GUINEA-BISSAU West Africa
GUYANA South America on a Budget
HOLLAND see Netherlands
HONDURAS Central America on a Budget
HUNGARY Budapest, Europe on a Budget, Hungary
ICELAND Iceland, Iceland Map
INDIA Goa, India, Kerala, Rajasthan, Delhi & Agra [1 title]
INDONESIA Bali & Lombok, South East Asia on a Budget
IRELAND Dublin Map, Europe on a Budget, Ireland, Ireland Map
ISRAEL Jerusalem
ITALY Europe on a Budget, Florence & Siena Map, Florence & the best of Tuscany, Italy, Italy Map, The Italian Lakes, Naples & the Amalfi Coast, Rome, Rome Pocket, Sardinia, Sicily, Sicily Map, Tuscany & Umbria, Venice, Venice Pocket
JAMAICA Jamaica, The Caribbean
JAPAN Japan, Tokyo
JORDAN Jordan
KENYA Kenya, Kenya Map

Download or buy Rough Guide **books**, **ebooks**, & **apps** online and instore

KOREA Korea, Seoul
LAOS Laos, South East Asia on a Budget
LATVIA Europe on a Budget
LESOTHO South Africa
LITHUANIA Europe on a Budget
LUXEMBOURG Belgium & Luxembourg, Europe on a Budget
MALAYSIA Malaysia, Singapore & Brunei [1 title], South East Asia on a Budget
MALI West Africa
MAURITANIA West Africa
MEXICO Mexico, Cancun & The Yucatan, Yucatan Peninsula Map
MONACO France, Provence & the Cote d'Azur
MONTENEGRO Montenegro
MOROCCO Europe on a Budget, Marrakesh Map, Morocco
NEPAL Nepal
NETHERLANDS Amsterdam, Amsterdam Map, Amsterdam Pocket, Europe on a Budget, The Netherlands
NEW ZEALAND New Zealand, New Zealand Map
NICARAGUA Central America on a Budget
NIGER West Africa
NIGERIA West Africa
NORWAY Europe on a Budget, Norway, Scandinavia
OMAN Oman
PANAMA Central America on a Budget, Panama
PARAGUAY South America on a Budget
PERU Peru, Peru Map, South America on a Budget
PHILIPPINES The Philippines, Southeast Asia on a Budget
POLAND Europe on a Budget, Poland
PORTUGAL The Algarve Map, Europe on a Budget, Lisbon Pocket, Portugal
PUERTO RICO The Caribbean, Puerto Rico
ROMANIA Europe on a Budget, Romania
RUSSIA Europe on a **BUDGET**, Moscow, St Petersburg
ST LUCIA The Caribbean
SCOTLAND Britain, Camping, Europe on a Budget, Scotland, Scottish Highlands & Islands
SENEGAL West Africa
SERBIA Montenegro, Europe on a Budget
SIERRA LEONE West Africa
SINGAPORE Malaysia, Singapore & Brunei [1 title], Singapore, Southeast Asia on a Budget
SLOVAKIA Czech & Slovak Republics, Europe on a Budget
SLOVENIA Europe on a Budget, Slovenia

SOUTH AFRICA South Africa, South Africa Map
SPAIN Andalucia, Andalucia Map, Barcelona, Barcelona Map, Barcelona Pocket, Europe on a Budget, Mallorca & Menorca, Mallorca Map, Spain
SRI LANKA Sri Lanka, Sri Lanka Map
SURINAME South America on a Budget
SWAZILAND South Africa
SWEDEN Europe on a Budget, Scandinavia, Sweden
SWITZERLAND Europe on a Budget, Switzerland
TAIWAN Taiwan
TANZANIA Tanzania, Zanzibar
THAILAND Bangkok, Southeast Asia on a Budget, Thailand, Thailand Beaches & Islands
TOGO West Africa
TRINIDAD & TOBAGO The Caribbean, Trinidad & Tobago
TUNISIA Tunisia
TURKEY Europe on a Budget, Istanbul, Turkey
TURKS AND CAICOS ISLANDS The Bahamas, The Caribbean
UNITED ARAB EMIRATES Dubai, Dubai & UAE Map [1 title]
UNITED KINGDOM Britain, Devon & Cornwall, England, Europe on a Budget, The Lake District, London, London Map, London Mini Guide, Scotland, Scottish Highlands & Islands, Wales, Walks in London & Southeast England
USA Boston, California, Chicago, Chicago Map, Florida, The Grand Canyon, Hawaii, Las Vegas, Los Angeles & Southern California, Miami & South Florida, Miami Map, New England, New Orleans & Cajun Country, New York City, New York City Mini Guide, New York Pocket, San Francisco, Seattle, Southwest USA, USA, Washington DC, Yellowstone & The Grand Tetons National Park, Yosemite National Park
URUGUAY South America on a Budget
US VIRGIN ISLANDS The Bahamas, The Caribbean
VENEZUELA South America on a Budget
VIETNAM Southeast Asia on a Budget, Vietnam
WALES Britain, Camping, Europe on a Budget, Wales
WORLD COVERAGE Earthbound, Great Escapes, Make the Most of Your Time on Earth, Make the Most of Your Time in Britain Ultimate Adventures

Start your journey at **roughguides.com**
MAKE THE MOST OF YOUR TIME ON EARTH™

ROUGH GUIDES

WE GET AROUND

ONLINE start your journey at roughguides.com

EBOOKS & MOBILE APPS

GUIDEBOOKS from Amsterdam to Zanzibar

PHRASEBOOKS learn the lingo

MAPS so you don't get lost

GIFTBOOKS inspiration is our middle name

LIFESTYLE from iPads to climate change

...SO YOU CAN TOO

BOOKS | EBOOKS | APPS

Start your journey at **roughguides.com**
MAKE THE MOST OF YOUR TIME ON EARTH™